Easy UPHOLSTERY
• STEP BY STEP •

Heather Luke

CHILTON BOOK COMPANY
Radnor, Pennsylvania

CONTENTS

For my husband, Don, who is always there to encourage, and to my children, Peter, Michael, and Lisa, for their tolerance and understanding.

Note: Where English terminology differs from the American, the English descriptions are given in brackets.

First published in the U.S. in 1994 by
Chilton Book Company, Radnor, Pennsylvania 19089

ISBN 0-8019-8630-3

Produced by Weldon Russell Pty Ltd
107 Union Street North Sydney NSW 2060 Australia
in association with Rosemary Wilkinson

Design: Patrick Knowles
Special photography: Mark Gatehouse
U.S. editor: Carol Parks
Illustrations: King & King

National Library of Australia Cataloging-in-Publication Data
Luke, Heather.

    Upholstery.

    Includes index.

    ISBN 0-8019-8630-3.

    1. Upholstery. I. Title.

746.95

Typeset by Fakenham Photosetting Limited
Produced by Mandarin Offset, Hong Kong
Printed in Hong Kong

A KEVIN WELDON PRODUCTION

FOREWORD

Covering, or repairing and re-covering, upholstered furniture with new fabric is something that most of us have, either from necessity or from curiosity, wanted to do at some stage. We have all had pieces of furniture with covers that have worn out, or which have become unsuitable due to a change of environment. This book seeks to encourage you to have a go at re-covering your own pieces of furniture, whether a large armchair or a small footstool, and to enjoy the creative reward and increase in confidence which will result. The step-by-step instructions have been carried out by skilled craftspeople, but demonstrated and adapted for the novice.

The basic upholstery and slipcover (loose cover) methods have been explained very thoroughly to enable you to apply the techniques learnt to any project. Your own pieces will probably not be exactly the same as any of the pieces shown: it is rare to find two chairs requiring identical treatments. However, they will have certain basic principles in common with the projects in this book. For instance, the method for re-upholstering a sprung armchair seat, making an over-stuffed seat, or an ottoman lid will be the same whatever the size and shape of the actual pieces. By studying the make-up of your piece, you will be able to find the appropriate methods in one or more of the projects in this book.

We have also shown how to use the twentieth century discoveries of foam, fiber, and staples to make your own headboards, screens, stools, and tables and to upholster a dining chair from the wooden frame. Modern techniques are easy to learn and produce rewarding results quickly.

Choosing the correct fabric for the job and the trimmings to add a special finish are important: ideas and direction are given in the style chapters. Furnishings rely on the interaction of colors, textures, and patterns to create style and atmosphere. Each home will have an individual style dependent on the personality of the occupants and the character of the house. We have photographed ten very different room settings and given explanations for the choice of upholstery in each case.

The overall aim is to show that, by combining care in the method with a creative choice of finish, you can produce exciting and individual results on your own pieces of furniture.

INTRODUCTION

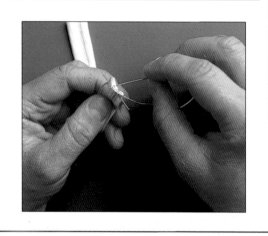

AN INTRODUCTION TO UPHOLSTERY

Traditionally upholstered furniture is constructed from basic hardwood frames covered with several layers of padding made from natural materials, supported on webbing and burlap (hessian), with or without springs, then covered with the fabric of your choice.

Much modern furniture consists of pieces of foam supported by burlap (hessian), plywood or even thick cardboard, on a much more roughly constructed frame. No matter what the construction, restoration is usually possible.

When buying a piece of furniture to restore, look at the basic shape. Arms, wings, and backs can be padded out, but it is not possible to change the shape. For example, a straight arm cannot be changed into a scroll arm by adding extra padding. It is the shape of the frame beneath all the padding that determines such a feature.

Joints in a chair tend to work themselves loose with wear and age. The glue actually deteriorates. Joints like this can be pulled further apart and wood glue applied to all the exposed surfaces prior to clamping the frame. Dowelling pegs in the joints can be replaced. Even pieces of the frame itself can be replaced. In a similar way, foam, plywood, and cardboard can all be replaced in modern furniture.

MEASURING AND ESTIMATING FABRIC QUANTITY

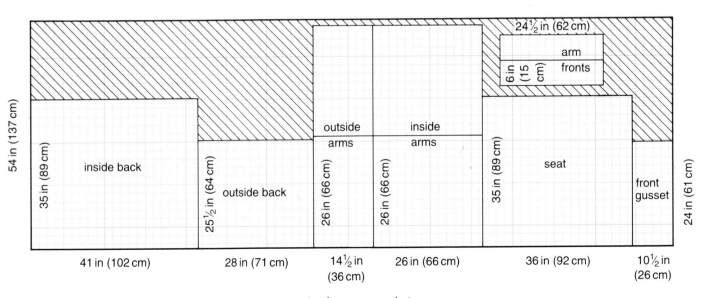

cutting layout – armchair

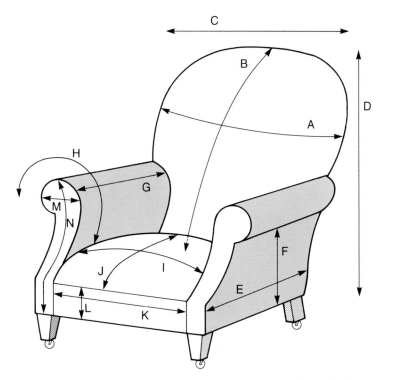

inside back	A width
	B length
outside back	C width
	D length
outside arm	E width
	F length
inside arm	G width
	H length over arm to seam
seat	I width
	J length
front gusset	K width
	L length
arm front	M width
	N length

sample armchair – measurements

Measuring for fabric must be done before starting work on the furniture, since the dimensions of the frame after stripping off the old materials are significantly less than those of the finished article.

Write down the measurements of each surface of the chair in both directions, as shown in the diagram, taking the widest point of that surface. For example, in the chair shown, the widest part of the arm is around the scroll at the front of the arm, while that of the inner back is just above the arms. Measure round the frame and down inside the chair where appropriate. For example, for the inside back piece, measure from the back of the frame at the top to the base of the frame at the bottom.

The next step is to plan the cutting layout. Note that upholstery fabrics are usually between 54 in (137 cm) and 60 in (152 cm) wide. It is sometimes possible to cut the fabric for two surfaces of a chair from one width of fabric, e.g. the two inside arms may be cut side by side, so the length measurement for the two surfaces need only be written down once. Similarly, the inside and outside back pieces can sometimes be cut side by side if you have a small chair, so just add into the total the longer of

the two back measurements. Small pieces, such as the fronts of arms, can usually be cut from fabric left over after the seat has been cut out. Extra fabric is needed for matching up patterns. As a rough guide, add 1 yard (1 meter) for matching up a chair and 2–3 yards (2–3 meters) for matching the pattern on a sofa. Make a pattern on graph paper before you cut any pieces out (see page 10).

The chair in the diagram takes $4\frac{1}{3}$ yards (3.93 meters) or $4\frac{1}{2}$ yards (4 meters) rounded up to the nearest half yard (meter). As a rough guide, add 1 yard (1 meter) to this if there is a pattern which will need to be matched on the chair pieces. Piping takes another 1 yard (1 meter) for the chair plus $\frac{1}{2}$ yard (0.5 metre) for every additional seat cushion, using either the same fabric as the chair or a contrast fabric. All the measurements shown in the cutting layout opposite have a 2 in (5 cm) seam allowance added.

Cut out all pieces as rectangles of fabric at this stage as shown in the cutting layout. They will not be cut to shape until they are being fitted to the chair. Always mark the center top and bottom of each piece after you have cut it out. Clip it with scissors – do not use pins, which could fall out.

STRIPPING

1 Turn the furniture upside down and protect any finished surfaces that could be damaged during stripping.

2 Using a mallet and chisel, remove all the tacks securing the fabric and webbing to the frame. Work with the grain of the wood to avoid splitting it, angling the chisel beneath each tack, prying it out with gentle taps from the mallet. There is no need to be too forceful since you risk damaging the frame and will certainly exhaust yourself. It can easily take a whole morning to strip one chair. As far as possible, remove all tacks, hammering in all those that refuse to budge. Staples should be dealt with using a special staple remover or a wide screwdriver.

3 Cut the springs out using a carpet knife. Test each one by putting it on a hard surface and pushing it down with your hand. It should compress vertically over itself. If it leans over to one side, discard and use a new one. Check the burlap (hessian) covering the springs, especially where it meets the frame of the chair and where the heads of the springs have been resting. Discard it if there are any weak areas.

4 Turn the furniture upright and remove the rest of the top cover. Keep all the pieces. You may need some for patterns for the new cover.

5 Remove the seat pad and burlap (hessian) covering the springs. If they are in good condition keep them for re-use.

6 Check the condition of the burlap (hessian) supporting the arm and back pads. Leave it in place if its condition is good. Otherwise remove it.

7 Check all the joints for movement. They should all be visible now. Re-glue loose ones using any good quality wood glue. Clamp them together and leave for 24 hours. Protect finished surfaces with tape or a wad of cloth under the clamp. Seek help from a carpenter if more extensive woodwork repairs are needed. The frame must be firm and in good condition before you start to reconstruct the upholstery. Use rough sandpaper to smooth off any splinters.

WOODWORM

This is caused by the wood-boring larvae of the common furniture beetle. The sign to look for is a series of tiny holes in the frame and legs. A live infestation will produce a shower of fresh wood dust when the chair is moved or worked on. Never bring a piece of furniture into your workshop or home until you have examined all the wood. The infestation readily spreads.

Treat the infestation even if it appears inactive. Use a commercial fluid. Work outside if possible, since this is a messy and smelly job, otherwise open doors and windows.

CLEANING AND POLISHING WOOD

Clean off areas where the wood is clogged with paint. To do this, use the finest possible steel wool dipped in mineral spirits (white spirit). Rub gently with a circular movement. Try this technique on a small unobtrusive area to see the effect.

Use wax polish with color added to disguise scuffs and scratches. There are several commercial brands which come in various wood colors. Give the wood several coats, allowing each coat to dry thoroughly before applying the next. Wax shoe polish (colored) is useful to cover up scratches.

WEBBING

*T*he webbing takes the weight of all the upholstery and consequently the weight of the person who uses the furniture. It should be really taut. Always renew webbing.

A chair with no springs has the webbing attached to the upper side of the frame, so all the upholstery has to be removed before the webbing can be replaced.

A chair with springs has the webbing on the underside of the frame. It is therefore possible to re-web such a chair without removing all the rest of the upholstery. Strip off the old webbing and cut it away from the springs with a carpet knife. The actual re-webbing process is exactly the same whether it is being put on the top or the underside.

Work out the number of strips required. The webbing strip is roughly three fingers wide. Place your fingers over the center point of the front of the chair to represent the first strip of webbing. Put three fingers of your other hand next to them – this gives you the distance between the strips.

Use both hands and work out to the sides of the frame. Having decided how many strips to use, mark their positions before you start work. Mark all four sides of the chair. Do not cut off the number of pieces you need; work from the roll of webbing and cut off after you have stretched and tacked each strip to the frame. Work as follows:

1 Line up the center of one end of the webbing with the center front of the chair.

2 Turn the end of the webbing under 1 in (2.5 cm) and place the folded edge, fold downward, over the center mark. Use four $\frac{1}{2}$ in (13 mm) tacks evenly spaced and hammer the tacks into the double thickness of webbing in the center of the rail. Pull the webbing toward the back of the chair.

3 Hold the webbing stretcher with the handle pointing away from you and with the ridge underneath.

4 Push a loop of webbing through the slit in the stretcher and push the peg through it.

5 Pull the stretcher over the back of the frame and wedge the ridge under the frame. The webbing must be taut and should "ping" like a drumhead when flicked with your finger. Adjust the loop of webbing and the peg until this feels right, then hammer three tacks into a single thickness of webbing, the outer two in the center of the rail, the third one farther back.

6 Cut off the webbing 1 in (2.5 cm) beyond the tacks, turn it back on itself and put in two more tacks, through the double thickness of webbing, avoiding the previous tacks.

7 Attach all the front-to-back pieces of webbing first, then attach the pieces across the frame, weaving them alternately under and over the front-to-back pieces.

SPRINGS

Coil Springs

Springs for traditional upholstery come in various sizes and gauges of wire. Seat springs need to be a heavier gauge as they take more weight than those in the back or arms. To judge the right size, place a spring on the webbing then add $2\frac{1}{2}$ in–3 in (6–8 cm) for the thickness of the seat pad.

Tension Springs

This type of spring runs across from the side rails of a chair, and is generally found on a modern chair. Metal plates with holes in them for the springs to clip into are fixed along the side rails.

Serpentine or Sinuous Springs

This is a zig-zag piece of wire fixed from the front rail to the back with special clips.

Innerspring (Meshed Top Spring) Units

These units are ready-made to fit the chair. The springs are enclosed in a wire mesh framework which is bolted onto the frame of the chair. It is not possible to replace individual springs: the whole unit has to be replaced.

SEWING IN COIL SPRINGS IN — TRADITIONAL UPHOLSTERY —

All springs are sewn in place at the base, some are also tied together at the top. Seating springs should be sewn and tied in place: the only exception being dining chairs. Their springs are usually only sewn in place. Arm springs are usually both tied and sewn in place.

1 Place the springs on the webbing. The distance between two springs and between the rows of springs should be the same. As a rough guide, allow between 3 and 4 in (7 and 10 cm) between the springs. The larger the springs, the greater the distance between them.

Springs are not symmetrical. The wire joint at the top and bottom of the springs should point in the same direction. Keep the springs well forward. This is the part of the chair which has the most use. Draw around the base of each spring, then remove all

but the back row. Always start sewing on the back row. If you work from the front and try to sew over the top of the springs the twine will become tangled.

2 Use a 4 in (10 cm) curved needle and spring twine. Attach the twine to the webbing using a slip knot, as shown in the diagram below.

3 Each spring is sewn to the webbing in three places. Take the needle down through the webbing on one side of the bottom ring of the spring, and bring it back through the webbing on

the other side of the ring. Pull the twine almost through but leave a small loop. Put the needle through the loop and pull tightly. Make two more knots equally spaced on the base of the spring before moving onto the next spring. There is no need to cut the twine between the springs. Fasten off making two or three stitches into the webbing when the twine runs out and start a fresh piece with another slip knot.

Use this process to attach springs both to the webbing and to the burlap (hessian) cover that goes over the springs.

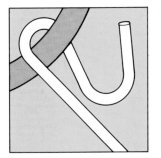
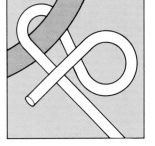

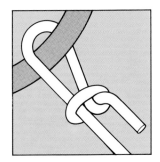

—— **TYING THE SPRINGS** ——

Springs are tied to each other with spring twine (laidcord), which is then attached to the rails of the chair by a tack.

1 Hammer a 1 in (25 mm) tack half its length into the chair rail opposite the center of the springs at the end of each row.

2 Measure and cut the length of twine needed for each row. This will be 1.75 times the distance between the two chair rails across the tops of the springs.

3 Attach a length of twine using a slip knot to the top ring of the spring level with the top of the seat rail.

4 Pull the twine back to the tack, wind it around twice and hammer in the tack.

5 Depress the front of the spring slightly. Take the twine up and over the top ring, bring it back through to the left of the vertical strand of twine, pass it over the vertical strand and up

under the top ring. This forms the knot.

6 Pass the twine over to the back of the ring and repeat the knot.

7 Take the twine to the next spring, keeping the distance at the tops of the springs the same as between the bases. Tie this spring in the same manner.

8 Repeat the process over the row of springs. Depress the last spring the same amount as the first one. Take the twine down to the tack, wind it around twice and hammer in the tack. Take the twine back to the spring ring, level with the frame, and finish by tying a secure knot with the end.

9 Work from front to back rails, then from side to side. Each spring should have four knots equally spaced on the top ring.

10 When all the springs are tied, they will all be depressed: those next to the rails more so than those in the middle. The overall shape of the springs should be slightly domed.

*T*ACKS AND *T*ACKING

*T*acks come in various lengths. The most frequently used are $\frac{1}{2}$ in (13 mm) for securing webbing and heavy-duty burlap (hessian), and $\frac{3}{8}$ in (10 mm) for lightweight burlap (hessian), muslin (calico), and top covers; 1 in (25 mm) tacks are used to anchor the twine when tying springs; $\frac{1}{4}$ in (6 mm) tacks are used with very delicate fabrics or in thin wood.

Always use a tack that is just adequate. You will need to vary the distance between tacks according to the amount of pressure the fabric has to take,

and according to the size of the tack. As a rough guide, tacks securing heavy-duty burlap (hessian) should be 2 in (5 cm) apart, while those securing lightweight burlap (hessian), muslin (calico), and top covers should be $1\frac{1}{4}$ in (3 cm) apart.

Always "temporary tack", i.e. drive the tacks in halfway, when securing muslin (calico) and top covers. They often need to be moved, since the fabric stretches while being fixed in place.

Do not try to re-use tacks. They are usually bent and will have lost their fine points.

CLOSURES AND FITTINGS

HOOK AND LOOP TAPE

This is used for fitting fabric to a hard surface. It should never be used as a closure. It looks ugly and makes a bulky join.

Machine stitch the hooked side to the fabric and staple the looped side to the wood or board. It is tempting to stitch the looped side to the fabric because it is easier on the fingers, but the tape will not function properly this way around.

The tape strips should be positioned so that the hooked side is against the looped side but very slightly above. Press the tape down hard, so that the hooks lock into the loops. Use the ½ in (13 mm) width for short lengths and 1 in (25 mm) for longer lengths needed for heavy fabric.

ZIPPERS

Use zippers for closures on all cushion covers. Match the color to the fabric background on scatter cushions. Use medium- to heavy-duty zippers on boxed cushions. These are available in long lengths in cream, white, and beige from upholstery suppliers. Never use for closing slipcover (loose cover) seams unless they are hand stitched inside on a placket, and therefore not visible.

To insert a zipper between two pieces of fabric, first open up the zipper fully. Press under ¾ in (2 cm) of the fabric, the length of the zipper. Pin this to one side of the zipper and machine stitch as close to the teeth as possible.

Close up the zipper. Fold the seam allowance under on the opposite piece of fabric. Place over the zipper, so that the previous stitching line is not visible. Pin to the zipper close to the opposite teeth and machine stitch in place. Open up the zipper slightly, so that the cushion pad, or whatever, can be pulled back through the opening.

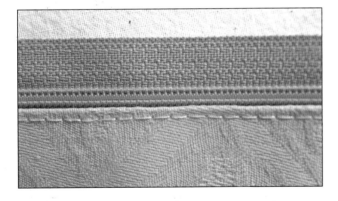 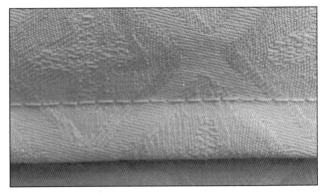

PLACKET WITH HOOKS AND EYES

Use this form of closure instead of a zipper for slipcovers (loose covers). Make up a placket so that one side lies over the other, and stitch purchased hooks onto the top side placket. Hand sew eyes in corresponding positions on the opposite side. Ties could be used in place of hooks and eyes.

T I E S

Ties are used to attach cushions to chairs or as closures on slipcovers (loose covers). They can be made a decorative feature by a careful choice of fabric, and they can be made in two ways.

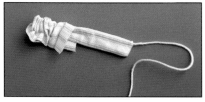

1 Cut a piece of fabric to the required length, plus seam allowances, and four times the finished width. Fold in half lengthwise, right sides together, enclosing a piece of piping cord which is slightly longer than the strip of fabric. Machine stitch along the short side to secure the cord, and along the length, just away from the center toward the raw edges.

Trim across the corner. Pull the cord through, thus turning right side out. Cut off the cord at the seam end and remove the remainder from inside.

Press. Turn under the raw edges at the open end and slipstitch together by hand to close.

2 Cut a strip of fabric to the required length and four times the finished width. Press in half lengthwise. Press each side in half again, so that the raw edges are enclosed in the middle. Open out. Press in ³⁄₈ in (1 cm) at one short end. Re-fold. Machine stitch along the length close to the open edges.

B o w s

Bows can be made in any size. Tie a piece of muslin (calico) or lining fabric to work out which size will best suit the piece to which it will be attached. Very wide tails can be made by tapering the fabric cuts, so that they are at their widest at the tail end and narrow toward the sash. Do not make the fabric too narrow at any point, the tie still needs fullness for the sash and excess fabric can be pleated at the back of the sash.

Allow plenty of fabric: it is often surprising how long bows need to be cut. See page 167 for further details.

1 Fold the top fabric with right sides together. Place the lining fabric pattern on top and cut out, allowing ⁵⁄₈ in (1.5 cm) seam allowance all around. Add piping to one of the pieces if desired.

2 Pin the bow pieces together along the seamline. Machine stitch all around the long sides and the front end. Trim the seams to exactly ³⁄₈ in (1 cm) all around. Trim across the corners.

3 Turn right side out. Pull the corners out to a point with a pin. Turn under the raw edges at the back end and slipstitch together.

4 Tie the bow so that the piece which comes up behind on the first tie will form the front band.

P i n s

Pins should be positioned to follow the seamline exactly, with the body straight and the heads pointing away from the direction from which the sewing machine will stitch. These pins will be removed one at a time to allow the stitching line to take their place.

Pins should also be placed at right angles to the stitching line at 2–4 in (5–10 cm) intervals. These will remain in place while stitching to prevent the layers of fabric moving.

Following a neat line of pins will achieve a straight stitching line and produce a much more professional finish than following a haphazardly pinned line.

PIPING

Piping cord is available commercially in a wide range of thicknesses, graded numerically according to the diameter of the cord. A no. 00 is the thinnest and a no. 7 the thickest generally available. The numbers correspond approximately to the metric measurement of the diameter, e.g. a 5 mm ($\frac{1}{4}$ in) diameter is designated as a no. 5 cord.

A heavy fabric will obviously produce a thicker cover, so the diameter of the cord can be varied to achieve the desired effect. The very narrow diameter cords can be used where decoration is needed but a thick edge of color is not.

Fabric for covering piping cord does not always need to be cut on the bias as is usually recommended. If the piece being piped is straight, e.g. a boxed cushion, then the piping covering may be cut straight. However, piping covering for curved pieces must be bias cut.

It is important that you have a piping or zipper foot on your sewing machine, which will allow you to stitch very close to the cord. Otherwise, whether the fabric is cut on the straight or on the bias, the casing will pucker.

Cut the fabric strips as long as possible to prevent unnecessary seams. Keep the width even, as you will use the casing to judge your seam allowance in many instances: use a ruler and pencil to mark the cutting lines. Always cut the ends on a 45° slant and sew the lengths together across the grain. Sewing straight across the ends will cause a thicker seam, with four layers of fabric together when the casing is folded over the cord.

The fabric to cover the cord should be cut wide enough to allow the fabric to fold over the cord plus double the chosen seam allowance. A $\frac{1}{4}$ in (5 mm) diameter cord will need approximately $\frac{3}{4}$ in (2 cm) of fabric, for example, so taking a seam allowance of $\frac{3}{4}$ in (2 cm), the width of the fabric strip will be:

$$[\tfrac{3}{4} \text{ in } (2 \text{ cm}) \times 2] + \tfrac{3}{4} \text{ in } (2 \text{ cm}) = 2\tfrac{1}{4} \text{ in } (6 \text{ cm}).$$

One of the easiest ways to ensure accuracy when stitching piping to the fabric to be decorated is to make sure that the seam allowance on the piping covering is exactly the same as the seam allowance on the piece to be piped.

PINNING PIPING ONTO THE FABRIC

Corners

Stop pinning at the seam allowance before each corner. Clip the casing fabric right up to the stitching line. Fold the piping sharply to make a 90° corner. The clip will spread out to show a square of fabric.

Curves

Clip into the casing fabric around inward curves to allow the casing to overlap and the piping to lie flat. If the fabric is bulky, cut notches.

Clip into the seam allowances around outward curves to allow the casing to spread to accommodate the curve and the piping to lie flat.

JOINING PIPING

1 Start to pin the piping to the top fabric at a point which will not be obvious when the article is made up.

2 Cut the other end of the piping cord approximately 1¼ in (3 cm) beyond the joining position.

3 Take out the stitches in the casing back to ¾ in (2 cm) beyond the joining position. Cut the inside cord away, so that the two pieces butt up.

4 Fold in ½ in (13 mm) of the raw edge. Fold this piece over the first piece and pin to secure. Double stitch over the join.

STITCHING PIPING INTO A SEAM

Trim the covered piping even with the raw edges, then pull a short length of piping cord from inside the casing and cut away the cord only, so that it will end at the seam stitching line. Cutting away the cord makes the seam less bulky. It also ensures that the piping cord is not held in position by the seam stitching line. This is important, because although the cord is pre-shrunk, it may shrink a little more with washing and, if sewn into a seam, it will cause puckering.

DOUBLE PIPING

Double piping is used as a decorative cover for the raw edges of fabric on an upholstered piece in place of gimp or other braid. It is also used when an edge is desirable but a contrast in color or texture is not, for example, at the bottom edge of a footstool or chair, where the fabric has been neatly turned under but the finished appearance is somewhat bare.

A double piping foot for the sewing machine is really needed to make the stitching easy. However, it can be stitched with an ordinary piping foot or by hand.

You will need to cut the piping strips just under three times the diameter of the two pieces of cord held together. Fold the fabric over the first piece of cord and stitch approximately ¼ in (6 mm) from the edge. Place the second cord against the first and fold the remainder of fabric over the top. Stitch through between the two cords.

CUTTING FABRIC

1 Check fabric for flaws and mark them. If the flaws are unacceptably noticeable, exchange the fabric as soon as possible after purchase. Manufacturers will not accept responsibility once the fabric has been cut.

2 Check that the pattern is not "off the grain", i.e. the horizontal placement of the motifs should follow the horizontal grainline. The allowed tolerance is 1¼ in (3 cm), but if it is more than ⅜ in (1 cm) off the grain, you will need to decide whether to keep the fabric or to try to return it.

3 Mark the right side of each piece with tacks or pins as it is cut and the direction of the pattern.

4 On printed fabrics cut away selvages. Snip into selvages on woven fabrics to allow some seam easement in case the fabric reacts to atmospheric changes.

5 Using your cutting layout, measure and mark with pins all the cuts required on the piece of fabric.

6 Cut carefully – always measure twice and cut once – and evenly. Cut square to the selvage. If the pattern repeat is off the grain, cut as nearly as possible to the pattern.

7 Leave pieces, overnight, with as few folds as possible to stabilize. Hang over a stair rail or table.

CHAIRS

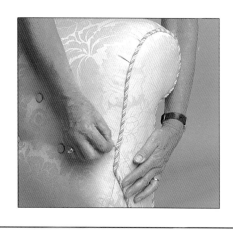

D ROP-IN S EAT

rop-in seats need to fit precisely. If they are too tight and have to be forced into the chair, they will eventually split the joints. If they are not tight enough, there is an ugly gap between the chair and the seat. Look carefully at the seat in the chair before you remove it and make a note of any alterations needed on the seat frame. If the chair is one of a set, number the chair and the seat. Even sets of matching chairs have small differences in size.

Materials

webbing
heavy-duty burlap (hessian)
horsehair
buttoning needle
twine
cotton batting (wadding)
muslin (calico)
½ in (13 mm) and ⅜ in (10 mm)
  tacks and tack hammer
top cover fabric
cambric (platform cloth)
marking pen
gimp pins

1 The padding on the seat of this chair has become compressed with use, and needs to be renewed. Strip everything off the frame. Keep the hair pad, discard everything else.

2 Check the joints for movement, and repair them if necessary (see page 12).

3 Lay the frame on a flat surface to check that it is not warped. If it is, this problem will need to be corrected by a professional carpenter.

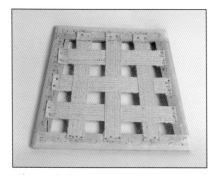

4 Mark the center front and back on the frame. Work out the number of strips of webbing needed (see page 13), and mark. The average size drop-in seat will need three strips in each direction. Working on the upper side of the frame, tack the back-to-front strips first, then weave the cross strips in alternately (see page 13). Check that the webbing "pings" when it is flicked with the finger. Try the frame in the chair. There should be an even gap all around at this stage. Plane off in the appropriate places any areas that were too tight when you examined it initially. Pad out, with thick cardboard, any areas where there were gaps. Make sure the frame is still level and that the webbing has not pulled it out of shape.

5 Measure the frame in both directions and add 2 in (5 cm) to both measurements. Cut a piece of heavy-duty burlap (hessian) to these measurements. Mark center front and back. Match centers at the back of the frame leaving 1 in (2.5 cm) of burlap

(hessian) protruding beyond the frame. Tack it on using $\frac{1}{2}$ in (13 mm) tacks at $1\frac{1}{4}$ in (3 cm) intervals. Stretch the fabric to the front of the frame, tack in the center front and work out to the corners, then stretch the sides and tack down. Trim the fabric to the shape of the frame leaving 1 in (2.5 cm) protruding all around the frame. Turn this over and tack down at 4 in (10 cm) intervals.

6 If you are using the old hair seat pad, spread some extra hair on the webbing and burlap (hessian) before putting the old pad back. Sew this down using the buttoning needle and twine. Sew right through the pad with stitches 4 in (10 cm) long. Sew rows of stitches 4 in (10 cm) apart, pulling the twine very tight between stitches. To make a completely new pad weigh out 1 lb (500 g) of horsehair. Spread it evenly over the webbing and burlap (hessian) and sew it down firmly to compress it.

Always use horsehair for seat pads. The seat will be softer.

7 Cover the horsehair with batting (wadding). Feather it off by hand around the edges. Do not let any hair or batting (wadding) come over the sides of the frame.

8 Measure for the muslin (calico) cover from under the frame and over the stuffing. Mark the center front and back and match up on the frame. Tack the back under the frame using $\frac{3}{8}$ in (10 mm) tacks. Check that the stuffing has not been pushed over the sides of the frame. Match the front centers. Smooth the muslin (calico) from the back to the front and put a tack in the center front. Work out to the front corners, smoothing the fabric and pulling it diagonally. Tack at $1\frac{1}{4}$ in

(3 cm) intervals. When you have tacked all across the front, the center tack may look as if it is holding the stuffing down too tightly. If so, release it and tack it again. Tack the sides of the muslin (calico) to the frame.

9 To tack and cut the corners, start at the back of the frame and put a tack at the top of the side of the frame 2 in (5 cm) in from the edge. Pull the muslin (calico) up and around onto the side of the back frame and secure with a gimp pin. Make a vertical fold down the line of the corner. Fold this back and cut away as much excess fabric as possible, then tack the folded corner down. Repeat on the other corners. Drive all the tacks in firmly and trim off any excess fabric around the frame. Try the seat in the chair. Check that no stuffing has slipped around onto the side of the frame, as this will give a bumpy appearance to the sides of the seat. Adjust if necessary.

10 Fit the top cover as for the muslin (calico). Match and center any pattern.

11 Tack a piece of cambric (platform cloth) onto the underside of the frame.

Over-Stuffed Dining Room Chair Without Springs

*T*hese instructions describe how to upholster a dining chair from the bare frame. The photograph shows the chair stripped off. All the joints have been checked for movement. The seat frame has been sanded down and prepared for the new upholstery.

Materials

webbing
burlap (hessian)
coir fiber
horsehair
cotton batting (wadding)
twine
$\frac{1}{2}$ in (13 mm) and $\frac{3}{8}$ in (10 mm)
  tacks and tack hammer
muslin (calico)
top cover fabric
black cambric (platform cloth)
stuffing regulator
buttoning needle
fabric glue
decorative braid
marking pen
webbing stretcher
gimp pins

1 Web the chair. Mark the center front and back on the upper surface of the rails of the chair. Fold under 1 in (2.5 cm) of the webbing. Place the middle of the folded end of the webbing over the center back mark and attach it to the rail using four $\frac{1}{2}$ in (13 mm) tacks.

2 Tighten the webbing using a stretcher. Point the handle of the stretcher away from you with its ridge underneath. Push a loop of the webbing through the slit in the stretcher and push the peg through the loop. Pull the handle toward you and wedge the ridge under the chair. Check the tension. The webbing should be taut and "ping" like a drumhead. Hammer in three tacks – the outer two nearer the front of the frame than the middle one. Cut the webbing $\frac{3}{4}$ in (2 cm) beyond the tacks and turn the end over. Hammer in two more tacks. Strips of webbing should be the width of three fingers apart. Place all the front-to-back pieces first, then weave in the cross pieces alternately over and under those at right angles.

3 Measure the chair for the heavy-duty burlap (hessian) which covers the webbing. Measure at the widest point front to back and side to side. Add 2 in (5 cm) in both directions. Mark the center front and back on the chair and the burlap (hessian). Match the centers at the back leaving a 1 in (2.5 cm) overlap and tack in place almost up to the back legs.

4 Match up the centers on the front rail. Stretch the burlap (hessian) tightly and tack down using $\frac{1}{2}$ in (13 mm) tacks, $1\frac{1}{4}$ in (3 cm) apart up to 2 in (5 cm) from the corners.

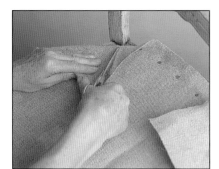

$\frac{3}{4}$ in (2 cm) from the line and bring it out from behind the ridge $\frac{3}{4}$ in (2 cm) above the line. Pull the twine through leaving a small loop under the line. Push the needle back into the pad $\frac{3}{8}$ in (1 cm) from the previous stitch, bring it out below the ridge and pass it through the loop of twine. Tighten the twine by pulling hard away from the stitch. Leave a 1 in (2.5 cm) gap and repeat the process. Use the regulator to pull the fiber into the roll between stitches.

5 Cut the burlap (hessian) around the back corners by turning back the corner and cutting from the point of the corner to the inner side of the back of the chair. Finish tacking the burlap (hessian) onto the back rail, then tack the sides starting at the back of the chair. The fabric should be as tight as you can stretch it. Trim off any excess evenly. Fold back the overlap and tack it down at 4 in (10 cm) intervals.

Mark the centers as before and match. Fold the burlap (hessian) under at the back and tack it onto the back edge of the chair using $\frac{3}{8}$ in (10 mm) tacks, $1\frac{1}{4}$ in (3 cm) apart. Tack the front, stretching it as you tack. Cut around the chair back as for the first layer of burlap (hessian). Fold under the sides and tack.

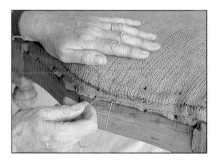

6 Use coir fiber to make the seat pad. Spread the fiber evenly and compress it to approximately 2 in (5 cm) deep. This small seat took 20 oz (570 g). It looks like a lot but it packs down. Always weigh hair and fiber if you are upholstering a set of chairs.

7 Measure in both directions over the fiber at the widest part of the chair for the next layer of burlap (hessian). Add on 4 in (10 cm) each way.

8 Stitch a firm edge (known as an edge roll) around the edge of the seat pad. To do this, use a marking pen to draw a line on the burlap (hessian) parallel to the frame measured from the worktable, then use the stuffing regulator to drag the fiber forward into the edges of the pad.

Use a 4 in (10 cm) curved needle and twine. Attach the twine with a slip knot $\frac{3}{4}$ in (2 cm) below the marked line. Push the regulator in along the line and pull the fiber forward to form a hard ridge. Push the curved needle under the ridge

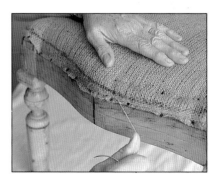

9 Stitch down the seat pad to the webbing and burlap (hessian) using a buttoning needle and twine. Push the needle right through the pad and make stitches 4 in (10 cm) long in rows 4 in (10 cm) apart.

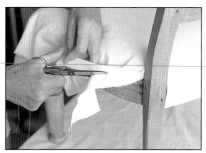

under the rails of the frame. Cut and mark the centers as for the burlap (hessian). Match the centers at the back and temporary tack the muslin (calico) under the chair. Match centers at the front. Pull the muslin (calico) with one hand, smoothing it forward with the other. Tack the center front under the chair. Tighten the calico diagonally to the front corners and tack the rest of the front in place. Cut the back corners as for the burlap (hessian). Fold the cut fabric around the corner following the grain, cut off the excess fabric and tack either side of the corner. Tack the rest of the sides down.

15 To complete the front corners, take the side fabric around the front leg. Cut the side fabric vertically at the start of the leg. Fold under and bring it around to the front of the leg. Put in 2 tacks $\frac{3}{4}$ in (2 cm) from the corner to hold the side fabric in place.

10 Cover the seat with a layer of horsehair 1 in (2.5 cm) thick (not compressed). This is to fill in the indentations made by the previous stitching. Catch the horsehair down loosely to the seat pad using the 4 in (10 cm) curved needle and twine.

13 Cut around the front leg at the side and front, wrap around the side and tack. Hammer in all the tacks.

THE TOP COVER

16 Cut vertically to the top of the frame at the side of the tacks.

11 Cover the horsehair with a layer of batting (wadding). Feather off by hand around the edges, so that the frame is still visible. Trimming with scissors leaves a hard edge, which will show through the top cover.

12 Measure the chair at its widest points for the muslin (calico) cover, allowing enough extra to tack

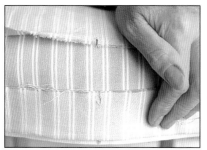

14 Measure and mark the top fabric as for the muslin (calico), being careful to center any pattern on the fabric. Tack the back and front down under the chair. Cut the back corners, trim the excess fabric and tack the sides down exactly as for the muslin (calico).

17 Cut around the front leg as for the side. Fold in the fabric to form the vertical line of the corner, then trim off the excess.

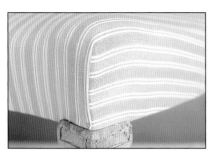

18 Fold the cut edge under and secure with a gimp pin. If the fabric is very thick it may be necessary to invisibly stitch the edge of the vertical fold to the side fabric (see page 60, step 11).

19 Cover the underside of the chair with cambric (platform cloth). Use $\frac{3}{8}$ in (10 mm) tacks. Cut around the legs as for the burlap (hessian).

20 Glue on the decorative braid. Put a dab of glue on the end of the back of the braid and turn it in. Use a gimp pin to attach the braid at the side of the chair. Apply more glue to the braid, then rub your finger along it to distribute it evenly. Press it in place around the sides and the front of the chair. Cut and turn the end of the braid in, securing it with a dab of glue. Secure

it to the chair with a gimp pin. Attach a piece of braid to the back of the chair using the same procedure.

DINING ROOM CHAIR WITH SPRUNG SEAT

A dining chair seat with springs incorporated will have a deeper seat than a chair without springs. This can be important when choosing a fabric for the top cover. Plain fabrics are no problem. Do make sure, however, that if your fabric has a large pattern, it is possible to put the center point of the pattern in the center of the chair and that there is still enough to cover the sides. If you are upholstering a set of chairs, it is more economical if two covers can be cut from one width of fabric. Check carefully before you buy.

Materials

webbing
springs
heavy-duty and lightweight
  burlap (hessian)
coir fiber
horsehair
cotton batting (wadding)
muslin (calico)
$\frac{1}{2}$ in (13 mm) and $\frac{3}{8}$ in (10 mm)
  tacks and tack hammer
spring twine (laidcord)
gimp pins
twine
strong thread
top cover fabric*
cambric (platform cloth)
buttoning needle
curved needle
liquid fabric cement (glue)
decorative braid

*see above

1 Measure the chair for the top cover.

2 Turn the chair upside down with the seat resting securely on another chair or table.

3 Protect the wood of the chair back if it is resting on the floor with a cloth or piece of foam.

4 Strip off the cambric (platform cloth) and the webbing, and loosen the top cover (see page 12). Cut the webbing away from the springs and discard. Never re-use old webbing. It is not possible to stretch it properly.

5 Turn the chair right side up. Take off the top cover.

6 Strip off the seat pad. If this is made of coir fiber or horsehair, keep it. It can probably be used again.

7 Strip off the heavy-duty burlap (hessian) covering the springs and discard. It has had a lot of wear from the movement each time the springs have been compressed.

8 Cut the old springs out and test each one by putting it on a flat surface and pushing it down over itself. If it leans over to one side, discard it and use a new one. It is not possible to produce a well-shaped seat if the springs are worn unevenly. Victorian and Edwardian chairs often have rather large springs which give an overblown look to the chair. If you are replacing all the springs, consider using new springs no more than 4 in (10 cm) high which will result in a seat more in proportion to the frame.

9 Check the joints of the chair for movement. The joints at the back are often loose as a result of people

balancing the chair on its back legs rather than using all four.

10 Prepare the frame for re-upholstery, i.e. treat woodworm and scratched areas; sand down rough areas (see page 12).

11 Mark the center front and back of the chair rails. Work out the number and position of the strips of webbing and mark them (see page 13). As the front of the chair is wider than the back, the strips of webbing will fan out slightly from the back to the front. Web the chair, attaching the webbing to the underside of the chair rails.

12 Turn the chair right side up and position four springs on the webbing, keeping them well forward. Position the bases of the front two 2½ in (6 cm) from the front rail of the chair with a gap of 4 in (10 cm) between them. Place the other two springs 4 in (10 cm) from the front two and 4 in (10 cm) apart. Put the join of the wire on the top ring in the same direction on each spring. Draw around the base of each spring, then remove the front row.

13 Each spring is sewn to the webbing in three places. Using a 4 in (10 cm) curved needle and twine, attach the twine to the webbing using a slip knot (see page 14). Take the needle through the webbing on one side of the base of the spring and pull the twine almost through, leaving a small loop. Bring the needle back up on the other side of the spring base, pass the needle through the loop and pull tight. Repeat

this twice more at equidistant points and then move on to the next spring. Fasten off by making several stitches into the webbing when all the springs have been sewn in place. It is not absolutely necessary to tie in the springs on a dining chair. If you wish to do so, follow the method described on page 15.

14 Measure for the heavy-duty burlap (hessian) cover from the back rail of the chair, over the springs to the front rail, then across the widest part of the chair, adding on 2 in (5 cm) extra in each direction to turn under. Cut, and mark center front and back. Match the centers at the back. Allow 1 in (2.5 cm) to protrude beyond the frame. Use ½ in (13 mm) tacks at ¾ in (2 cm) intervals and tack the burlap (hessian) to the frame to within 1¼ in (3 cm) of the back corners. Match center fronts. Pull the fabric forward and tack the center front down. You must pull very hard. This cover must be really tight. Tack to within 2 in (5 cm) of the front corners.

15 To cut the burlap (hessian) around the back of the chair, fold the two back points forward, then cut from the point to the inside edge of the back of the chair. Pull the two cut sides around the corner and tack them down. The fabric must be really tight to the wood: stuffing from the seat pad will fall through if there is a gap. Tack the rest of the sides down. Leave 1 in (2.5 cm) extending beyond the rails all around the chair. Trim off the excess. Fold the rest over and tack at 4 in (10 cm) intervals.

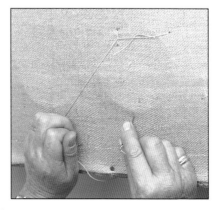

16 Sew the tops of the springs in place in exactly the same way and in the same pattern as on the webbing, checking that they are evenly spaced. The burlap (hessian) cover should feel very tight and be slightly domed.

17 Separate the layers (there are usually two) of the seat pad, if it is re-usable. Remove all the old tacks and shake it to get rid of dust and dirt. Old seat pads are usually compressed in the middle. Spread some new horsehair or coir fiber over the springs and burlap (hessian) to fill any dips before you replace the pad. When the seat feels even and level, tack it down on the outer edges of the rails all around the chair. Take the buttoning needle and twine and sew the pad down. Avoid the springs and bring the needle down through the gaps between the strips of webbing. Use stitches 4 in (10 cm) long with 4 in (10 cm) between the rows of stitching. Pull the thread taut as you sew, so that the pad is tightly stitched down.

If it is not possible to re-use the seat pad, add a layer of coir fiber following the method described on page 25.

18 Fill in the indentations before replacing the second pad. Check with your hands that the seat feels even all over. Use more hair if necessary. Weigh all extra coir fiber and horsehair if you are working on a set of chairs, so that they all will look alike.

19 Catch down the horsehair loosely using a 4 in (10 cm) curved needle and twine.

20 Cover the horsehair with batting (wadding). Feather off by hand around the edges. You should still be able to see the sides of the frame.

21 Measure for the muslin (calico) cover from under the chair and over the batting (wadding) in both directions at their widest parts. Cut and mark the centers. Line up the back center and temporary tack under the back rail using ⅜ in (10 mm) tacks.

22 Line up the center fronts. Pull the muslin (calico) toward the front with one hand, smooth it with the other and temporary tack under the front rail.

23 Cut the back corners as for both layers of burlap (hessian). Trim off the excess fabric, then tack down the rest of the back and sides.

24 To finish the front corners, cut the muslin (calico) around the legs at the front and side. Bring the sides around to the front and tack, then smooth the front from the center toward the corner and back around the side. Tack in place.

25 Measure for the top cover as for the muslin (calico), being careful to center any pattern. Tack on the back and front. Cut the back corners, fold the cut fabric back on itself and trim off the excess. The fold should run along the grain of the fabric. Finish tacking the back and sides.

26 Cut around the legs at the sides, fold in the raw edge, bring the side around to the front and tack. Make a vertical cut to the top of the frame beyond the tacks.

27 Cut around the leg at the front. Make a vertical fold to form the corner. Turn the fold back on itself and

trim off the excess fabric. The cut should meet the vertical cuts on the side fabric. The thicker the fabric the more you should trim off in order to reduce the bulk.

28 Turn in the raw edges and secure the corner with a gimp pin. Sew the corner fold down invisibly if the fabric is thick (see page 60, step 11).

29 Tack the cambric (platform cloth) under the chair (see page 27, step 19).

30 Glue on the decorative braid (see page 27, step 20).

MODERN DINING ROOM CHAIR

*T*he seat of this dining chair is made with a rubberized hair pad and a paper roll. Chairs of this size and style are often used in restaurants and other public places where the furniture has to take a lot of wear. Choose a hard-wearing top fabric, such as this dobby weave. A loose cover looks as good as an upholstered one with the advantage that it is removable for cleaning (see page 135).

Materials

webbing
heavy-duty burlap (hessian)
flanged paper edge roll
coir fiber
rubberized hair 1 in (2.5 cm) thick
cotton batting (wadding)
muslin (calico)
$\frac{3}{8}$ in (10 mm) and $\frac{1}{2}$ in (13 mm)
   tacks and tack hammer
staples and staple gun
top cover fabric
cambric (platform cloth)
buttoning needle
twine
piping
gimp pins

1 Web the seat and the back of the chair (see page 13), placing the webbing strips no more than 2 in (5 cm) apart.

2 Measure and cut out a heavy-duty burlap (hessian) cover for the seat and back of the chair, allowing 2 in (5 cm) extra all around on both pieces. Mark the centers of the burlap (hessian) at the top and bottom.

3 Work on the seat first. Match up the back centers on the chair and the burlap (hessian), with 2 in (5 cm) extending beyond the back of the frame, and tack in place using $\frac{1}{2}$ in (13 mm) tacks, 2 in (5 cm) apart. Tack to within 2 in (5 cm) of the corners.

4 Match up the front centers of the chair and the burlap (hessian). Tack to the chair, pulling it very tight. Tack to within 4 in (10 cm) of the front corners.

5 Cut to fit around the back of the chair. Cut from the back point of the burlap (hessian) toward the inner edge of the back. Pull it around the sides of the back and tack it down.

6 Finish tacking down the front and sides. Trim off the excess leaving 2 in (5 cm) to turn over and tack down.

7 Tack the burlap (hessian) cover onto the back of the chair, starting at the bottom.

8 Tack the flanged paper edge roll around the seat of the chair. This is used instead of stitching a firm edge. Use $\frac{1}{2}$ in (13 mm) tacks, 2 in (5 cm) apart.

9 Fill the area inside the roll with coir fiber 1 in (2.5 cm) deep (compressed). Sew it firmly down through the burlap (hessian) using the buttoning needle and twine.

10 Cut a piece of rubberized hair large enough to overhang the roll by $\frac{3}{8}$ in (1 cm) all around. Cut a small piece out of it, so that the hair fits tightly around the back corners.

11 Cover the rubberized hair with batting (wadding). Trim it off by hand 1 in (2.5 cm) above the lower edge of the frame.

12 For the muslin (calico) cover, measure from under the frame and over the filling at the widest part of the frame. Cut to these dimensions. Mark the center front and back.

13 Match up the centers of the muslin (calico) and the frame at the back of the chair. Temporary tack in place using $\frac{3}{8}$ in (10 mm) tacks, then match up the centers at the front and put in the center tack. Pull the muslin (calico) diagonally toward the corners and tack the front down to within 4 in (10 cm) of the front corners.

14 Cut the muslin (calico) at the back on each side even with the inner edge of the back. Push the rest of the back edge through to the back of the seat and tack it down. Leave the side pieces of the corners until the back of the chair has been upholstered.

15 Tack the rest of the sides down. Cut the muslin (calico) to fit around the front leg. Tuck the raw edge under and pull the muslin (calico) around the leg and tack it above the leg 1 in (2.5 cm) in from the corner.

16 Cut the muslin (calico) around the front leg. Tuck the raw edges under to make a vertical fold exactly on the corner. Turn the fold back. Cut off the excess muslin (calico) under the fold. Return it to the corner and tack it down using a gimp pin.

17 Repeat steps 12 to 16 to fit the top cover, taking care to center any pattern.

18 Cut a piece of rubberized hair to the shape of the back. Staple it in place and trim off any that overlaps the frame.

19 Cover the hair with batting (wadding) trimmed off to the edge of the frame.

20 Cut the muslin (calico) cover. Mark the centers at the top and bottom. Tack onto the back of the bottom rail of the backrest, matching the center points. Cut at the sides to fit around the rail. Push through between the back and the seat. Pull up and tack it onto the back of the top rail of the back, matching the centers of the muslin (calico) and frame. Pull the

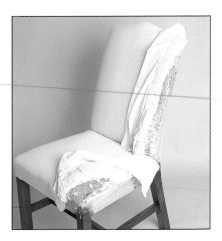

fabric diagonally toward the top corners and tack down the rest of the top back. Tack the sides down.

21 Repeat step 20 to fit the top cover, taking care to match and center any pattern.

22 To finish the side back corners on the seat of the muslin (calico) and top cover, clip the fabric around the corner and tack it on the back of the chair. Cut around the back legs and turn the raw edge under.

23 Tack burlap (hessian) on the back of the chair.

24 Tack piping around the sides and across the top of the back of the chair back.

25 Pin and sew the top cover to the back.

26 Tack cambric (platform cloth) on the underside of the chair.

ARMCHAIRS

*F*our very different shapes of armchairs are shown in the photographs. Each has a special feature which is not shared by the others.

The basic instructions describe the re-upholstering of a small armchair without wings or scroll arms. These are covered in the following three chairs which also show a rounded seat front, an independent front row of springs, and a wing and arm combined. The special features are listed by the photo of each chair and the instructions are given there. Refer to the basic directions to re-upholster the rest of the chair.

As far as the upholstery is concerned, a sofa is just a larger version of an armchair. The fabric on the inner and outer back and on the seat will probably need to be made up of more than one width. In this case, use the full width of the fabric for the center panel. Match the pattern carefully and machine stitch the extra fabric needed at each side of this panel.

Cushions on either a sofa or chair should be made following the instructions for box cushions (see page 115).

Suggested fabrics

Most armchairs look better upholstered in a fabric that has some sort of pattern, either one that is in the weave of the fabric, e.g. damask, or linen and cotton mixes, which give the effect of a one-color fabric, or one where there is a background color with other colors added to form the pattern.

When choosing a top cover fabric take into account:

a How much wear the chair will have.

b Its position in the room, e.g. whether it is going in a dark corner or sunlight.

c Whether there are pets in the house: dogs and cats can ruin loose-weave fabrics very quickly.

d The pattern repeat. You may need almost double the quantity of fabric if it has a large pattern. Small all-over designs and fabrics with heavy grain are probably the easiest to work with. Stripes and checks should be left to the more advanced upholsterer. Choose a fabric with some "give" in it, if it has to be stretched around curves on a chair.

SMALL ARMCHAIR

Materials

webbing	strong thread
springs – different gauges for the seat and back	1 in (25 mm), ½ in (13 mm) and ⅜ in (10 mm) tacks and tack hammer
heavy-duty and lightweight burlap (hessian)	top cover fabric
coir fiber	cambric (platform cloth)
horsehair	4 in (10 cm) curved needle
cotton and polyester batting (wadding)	buttoning needle
muslin (calico)	decorative braid
spring twine (laidcord)	liquid fabric cement (glue)
twine	gimp pins

1 Measure the chair for the new top cover (see page 11).

2 Turn the armchair upside down and strip off the cambric (platform cloth), the webbing, and the top cover where it is attached to the underside of the frame (see page 12).

3 Cut the springs away from the webbing and from the burlap (hessian). Test each spring by putting it on a flat surface and pushing it down over itself. If it leans over to one side, discard and use a new one.

4 Turn the chair right side up. Remove the seat layer by layer right down to the frame. You may be able to use some of the layers again. Keep everything at this stage.

5 Remove the inner and outer top cover from the arms and back of the chair. Keep them to use as patterns for the new cover.

6 Remove the pads on the arms and backs and set aside. Strip off the burlap (hessian) and webbing on the back and arms. Test the springs from the back in the same way as for the seat. Not all chairs have these springs. They give a softer feel to the back of a chair.

7 Examine the joints of the frame for movement; also check that there is no woodworm. Treat both these things if necessary (see page 12).

8 The back and arms of the chair are re-upholstered first. It is easier to tack everything down and cut parts to fit when the seat is not in place.
Replace any webbing strips on the back and arms, following the method for webbing a seat (see page 13). Avoid the old tack holes. The strips should feel just as taut as those for a webbed seat.

9 Sew the springs back onto the webbing on the back of the chair (see page 14). There is no need to tie the springs to the frame as you would on a seat.

10 Measure and cut a heavy-duty burlap (hessian) cover and tack it onto the upper and lower rails of the arm. Tack it to the front of the arm but leave the back free, as you will need to tuck all the other layers of upholstery through this gap.

11 Measure, cut, and tack the burlap (hessian) onto the front of the back, covering the springs, using $\frac{1}{2}$ in (13 mm) tacks. Keep it taut. Leave a small gap where the arm rail joins the back. Sew the springs to the burlap (hessian) using a 4 in (10 cm) curved needle and twine, and stitching at three points on each spring (see page 14). Check that the shape of the back is even. Adjust if necessary.

12 Examine the horsehair pads to see if they are re-usable. If they are not, follow the directions on page 54, steps 6–7. Remove all the old twine and give them a good shake to get rid of dust. It is even possible to wash the pads. Put them in a pillow case and wash on a delicate cycle in the washing machine. Air-dry them thoroughly before using them again. Before you replace the pads spread a layer of horsehair or coir fiber on the new burlap (hessian), particularly in the middle and top of the back and the tops of the arms. These are the main pressure areas and will have become compressed.

13 Stitch the new stuffing and the pads in place, using the buttoning needle and twine. Sew right through the pads. The stitches should be 4 in (10 cm) long in rows 4 in (10 cm) apart. Avoid the springs and webbing.

14 Some armchairs, usually the larger ones, have two layers of horsehair on the front of the back and arms. If there are two, the first layer will be covered with a lightweight burlap (hessian). (If there is only one layer, proceed to step 16.) Replace this if it is worn. Measure over the pads from under the lower rails, over the stuffing, onto the back of the upper rail. Measure across the pad at its widest part, allowing 4 in (10 cm) extra to turn under. Tack the burlap (hessian) onto the back of the lower rail first, turning the raw edges in, then pull it up and over the top rail and tack. This burlap (hessian) does not need to be pulled tight like the previous layer. Tack the front. Depending on the shape of the arms and the back, e.g. if it is a scroll or straight, you may need to stitch an edge roll along the side (see page 37).

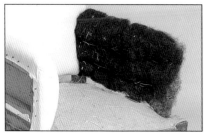

15 Cover the burlap (hessian) with a thin layer of hair (not compressed). Catch down in a few places using the 4 in (10 cm) curved needle and twine.

16 Cover the hair with a layer of burlap (hessian) tacked down as before, then add a layer of batting (wadding). Feather off the edges by hand.

17 Measure for the muslin (calico) lining at the widest parts of the inside back and arms and mark the center of fabric and chair.

18 Tack the inside back to the back of the lower rail. Pull it up and over the top rail smoothing it with the other hand as you pull. Temporary tack the center, then work out to the corners, pulling the fabric diagonally. Push the muslin (calico) into the gap between the inside back and the arm. Feel where the wood of the top rail of the arm joins the back frame and mark the center on the back muslin (calico). Pull the muslin (calico) out of the gap, fold it back on itself and cut either side of the mark. This cut piece should be the width of the upper arm rail. Tuck this piece of muslin (calico) back through the gap. This will be tacked down later.

19 Tack the side of the muslin (calico) up to the top corner. Fold the corner and cut off the excess fabric. Feel where the bottom rail of the arm joins the back frame and make another cut on the muslin (calico) level with it. Tuck the muslin (calico) through the gap between the arm and the inside back and tack down. Cut the muslin (calico) on the lower back rail and finish with a free-hanging square of muslin (calico). Push this between the lower arm rail and the base of the seat, and tack. Tack the other side of the muslin (calico) to the back in the same manner.

20 Tack the muslin (calico) onto the arms. Start under the bottom rail, then pull it up and over the top rail. Cut in the same manner as the inside

back to fit around the rail of the arm. Tack the front of the arm in place, starting at the bottom and working up. Tack it right up to the corner. Fold the fabric on the top of the arm at the front corner, so that it is in line with the front of the arm. Trim off the excess fabric inside the fold and tack the fold down. Leave the muslin (calico) free at the back of the arm.

21 The top cover is applied in exactly the same way as the muslin (calico). Match up any patterns. Do not turn in the raw edges, they will be covered by the fabric on the outside of the chair.

22 Now work on rebuilding the seat. Re-web and sew in the springs. The size will depend on the size of the armchair. The larger the chair, the larger the springs. An average armchair would have three rows of three springs. Place them well forward and point the joins in the wire on the top ring in the same direction (see page 14). Tie down the springs (see page 15).

23 Measure, cut, and tack down a heavy-duty burlap (hessian) cover over the springs (see page 29). Sew the springs to the burlap (hessian).

24 Use the old seat pad with extra coir fiber underneath to make it level, or cover the burlap (hessian) with a 2 in (5 cm) (compressed) layer of coir fiber to make a new seat. Tuck plenty down the sides of the chair and along the front of the seat.

25 Measure from the top of the back rail over the stuffing to the top of the front rail and across the widest part of the seat. Add 4 in (10 cm) in each direction to tuck under. Cut a piece of lightweight burlap (hessian) to these measurements. Mark centers and match. Tack the back first, turning the raw edges under. Pull the burlap (hessian) forward, and, using $\frac{3}{8}$ in (10 mm) tacks, tack onto the edge of the front rail. Push in more coir fiber if the front slopes too much. Cut the burlap (hessian) to fit around the back of the chair and also where the front arm joins the seat frame. Turn all the raw edges under and finish tacking down the burlap (hessian).

26 Sew an edge roll across the front of the chair (see page 25).

27 Use the buttoning needle and make stitches 4 in (10 cm) long in rows 4 in (10 cm) apart over the rest of the seat.

28 Cover the seat pad with a layer of horsehair 1¼ in (3 cm) deep (not compressed). Sew with a few small stitches to the pad below using the 4 in (10 cm) curved needle.

29 Cover the hair with a layer of cotton batting (wadding).

30 For the muslin (calico) cover, measure from under the frame and over the seat. Cut the muslin (calico) to these measurements. Mark and match centers. Tack onto the back

of the frame first. Pull and smooth to the front and tack down. Cut the back corners and around the arms, then tack down. There should be no gaps between the seat and arms: add more horsehair under the batting (wadding) if there are. Cut and tack down the corners (see page 26).

31 Cut the top cover for the seat as for muslin (calico), being careful to match up any pattern on the seat and back. Tack in place and cut as for the muslin (calico) around the back and arms. Invisibly sew the front corners.

32 Check all the inside top covers. Tighten them if necessary. Tack down and turn in all the pieces pushed through the gaps between the arms and back. Pull the loose end of the heavy-duty burlap (hessian) over these turnings, turn in the raw edges and tack down. Generally neaten the outside.

33 Tack the burlap (hessian) to the outside back of the back and the arms, to support the top cover. Add a layer of polyester batting (wadding).

34 Measure and cut the muslin (calico) for the outside arms. Turn the chair upside down, resting on its arms. Line up the fabric on the underside of the top arm rail, keeping the grain of the fabric straight. (Outside arms are often deeper at the front than the back.) Keep the fabric taut. Line up the back tack strip along the outer edge of the rail. Using ½ in (13 mm) tacks, tack in place through the strip and fabric. Turn the fabric over and tack under the bottom rail of the chair. Tack the sides.

35 Back tack the outside back cover in place along the back edge in the same way as the arms. Turn the fabric over and tack the bottom under the lower edge of the chair. Turn the sides in, pin in place and sew invisibly, finishing with a gimp pin.

36 Measure and cut the top cover fabric for the outside back and arms and attach in the same way as for the muslin (calico). If any tacks are visible at the front sides, then sew invisibly instead. Glue or sew on braid to cover the join.

37 Tack cambric (platform cloth) over the underside of the chair.

38 Sew or glue on any decorative braid that is being used.

ARMCHAIR VARIATIONS

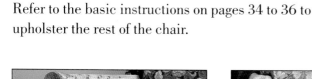

LARGE ARMCHAIR

The special features of this chair are:

- the scroll arm and back
- the rounded front on the seat.

Refer to the basic instructions on pages 34 to 36 to upholster the rest of the chair.

1 Tack a layer of heavy-duty burlap (hessian) on the inside of the frame of the arm.

2 Cover with coir fiber 2 in (5 cm) deep (compressed).

3 Cover the fiber with lightweight burlap (hessian). Using ⅜ in (10 mm) tacks, tack onto the upper and lower arm rails and around the front of the arm. Leave the back free.

4 Sew an edge roll on the front of the arm using a buttoning needle and twine (see page 25, step 8). Use the regulator along the side of the arm to pull the stuffing and burlap (hessian), so that they overhang the top rail slightly.

5 Cover the arm with horsehair, filling in all the hollows made by stitching. Catch down loosely with a 4 in (10 cm) curved needle in a few places and cover with cotton batting (wadding).

6 Cover the arm with muslin (calico). Tack it onto the back of the bottom rail of the chair first. Pull it up and over the arm. Tack it under the top rail. Cut it at the back to accommodate the arm rails (see page 35).

7 At the front edge of the arm, tack in place working upward from the bottom to 1 in (2.5 cm) beyond the start of the outer curve. Start the pleats from here and work around to the outer edge of the scroll.

8 Cut and fit the top fabric for the arm in the same way.

9 Back tack the outer arm top fabric in place under the top rail of the arm (see page 36, step 34). Tack the bottom under the chair. Tack the side back down. Tack the front side down as far as the seat, then sew the rest, as tacks would be visible.

10 Cut out the pieces of top fabric to make the pads on the front of the scroll, allowing 1 in (2.5 cm) to turn under. The pads can either have piping sewn onto them before they are attached to the chair, or they can have cord sewn on afterwards to cover the seam. Pin them in place over a small pad of cotton batting (wadding) to fill them out. Use a 2 in (5 cm) curved needle and matching strong thread to attach them to the chair. If using cord, bind the ends with sticky tape to stop it fraying and tuck this under the pad at one corner. Sew the cord around the pad. Before cutting off the cord allow enough to tuck under the pad, put more tape on the cord and cut through the middle of this. Tuck in the end and finish sewing.

Rounded Front on the Seat

11 Measure for the muslin (calico) from the back rail of the chair over the seat to 1 in (2.5 cm) below the roll. Measure the width at the widest point across the front. Cut the muslin (calico) to these measurements.

12 Cover the horsehair with a layer of cotton batting (wadding) trimmed by hand.

13 Mark and match the center back and front on both chair and fabric. Tack the center back down, then tack sideways in both directions to within 4 in (10 cm) of the back corners. Cut the corners and tack down the rest of the back, using $\frac{3}{8}$ in (10 mm) tacks.

14 Pull the fabric forward and pin it to the base of the chair under the roll. Fold the side fabric back onto the seat. Make a cut in the fold on a line even with the point where the back edge of the arm joins the side rail of the seat, then push the side fabric down between the arm and the seat. Tack the side fabric down. Pull the rest of the side fabric down between the front of the arm and the seat, clipping it if necessary around the arm. Sew down the front of the seat cover using a 4 in (10 cm) curved needle and twine. Start in the middle of the chair, work to one side, back to the middle, out to the other side, and then back to the middle. This way of stitching gives the effect of a continuous row of stitches.

15 Repeat steps 11, 13 and 14 for the top cover.

16 Cover the fabric below the roll with a thin layer of horsehair, stitch it down loosely and cover it with cotton batting (wadding).

17 Measure and cut out the top cover for the front section below the roll. Sew piping along the top of the piece. This will sit in the join between the seat corner and the front piece of fabric.

18 Pin the front piece in place. Check the measurements from the base of the chair as you pin. Sew it in place invisibly. To do this, stitch into the back of the piping and into the fabric on the seat alternately. Tack the bottom of the piece under the chair, then tack the sides. Check that the front piece is the same depth all around the front. Adjust if necessary.

LARGE WING CHAIR

The special features of this chair are:
- the separate wing and arm
- the independent row of springs along the front of the chair.

The chair in the photograph also has a separate matching cushion.

The reason for having a row of springs tied only to themselves and to a piece of cane or wire and not tied to the rest of the seat springs is to give a softer but firm edge to the chair.

Refer to the basic instructions on pages 34 to 36 to upholster the rest of the chair.

The Wing

1 Tack the burlap (hessian) on the inner side of the wing.

2 Cover with coir fiber 2 in (5 cm) deep (compressed).

3 Cover the fiber with lightweight burlap (hessian) tacked onto the edge of the wing at the front and top and to the rail of the arm at the bottom. Make two cuts in the burlap (hessian) at the back edge of the wing, the upper one even with the lower edge of the top rail of the wing and the lower one even with the top of the arm rail. Push the larger flap sideways through the gap between the wing and the back of the chair. Push the smaller flap (at the bottom) through the gap in the back of the chair where the arm rail is attached. Sew an edge roll around the front of the wing (see page 25, step 8).

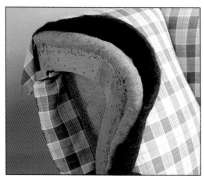

4 Cover the wing with horsehair sewn down loosely using a 4 in (10 cm) curved needle, then cover with cotton batting (wadding).

5 Cut a muslin (calico) cover and tack in place, keeping the grain straight. Tack the bottom of the muslin (calico) onto the rail of the arm first,

then pull it up and over onto the top of the back of the wing. Cut the flaps to tuck through as for the burlap (hessian). Clip the lower edge of the muslin (calico) to fit it around the curve where the wing and arm join. Pleat the muslin (calico) neatly around the front edge of the wing.

6 Put the top fabric in place using the same method.

7 Cut the outer wing and pin it in place around the top and front of the wing. Sew it down using a 2 in (5 cm) curved needle and strong thread. Tack the lower and back side edges.

Independent Row of Springs on the Front of the Chair———

1 Choose a size of spring which when balanced on the front rail of the chair is level with the springs on the webbing.

2 Attach the springs to the rail by threading a piece of webbing over the bottom rings. Put in ½ in (13 mm) tacks on either side of the ring at four different points.

3 Attach a piece of cane or wire to the springs using twine. To do this, cut a piece of twine 20 in (0.5 meter) long for each spring. Start with a slip knot, then use blanket stitch. Tie the short ends of the twine together.

4 Tie the springs together (see page 15), taking the twine (laidcord) down to a large tack between each pair of springs.

5 For a heavy-duty burlap (hessian) cover, measure from the back rail of the chair, over the large springs. Push the tape measure down between the large and small springs, then up and over the cane or wire to the bottom of the front rail of the chair. Measure across the front row of springs for the width measurement and add 2 in (5 cm) in each direction to turn under. Tack the back and sides as for the dining room chair (see page 29). Push the burlap (hessian) down into the gap behind the

front row of springs. Bring it up and over the front cane or wire and tack it onto the front of the seat frame.

6 Tack a piece of webbing across the chair in the gap between the springs to hold the fabric down.

7 Blanket stitch the burlap (hessian) to the length of cane or wire using the 4 in (10 cm) needle and twine. Sew the burlap (hessian) to the springs (see page 14).

8 Stuff the gap between the springs with coir fiber.

9 Make the seat pad in the same way as for the small armchair (page 35), sewing the burlap (hessian) at the front to the cane or wire instead of tacking it to the frame. Sew the edge roll in the usual way (see page 25).

10 Cover the seat pad with hair, cotton batting (wadding) and muslin (calico). Sew the muslin (calico) to the burlap (hessian) just under the cane or wire.

11 Fix the top cover in place. This will also be sewn to the burlap (hessian) just under the cane or wire.

12 Pad out the area under the cane or wire with a thin layer of horsehair sewn on loosely. Cover with cotton batting (wadding).

13 Measure for the top cover from the cane or wire to the bottom edge of the chair frame. Add 2 in (5 cm) to turn under. Turn the top edge in and pin it to the top cover of the seat just above the cane or wire. Put in a tack at each end. Tack the bottom of the fabric under the chair frame. Check that the fabric is the same depth all along the front of the chair, then sew it in place invisibly. Tack the fabric down at the sides. Sew a piece of cord along this seam attached with a tack at each side of the chair. Alternatively, a piece of contrast piping can be sewn to the fabric before it is sewn to the chair, as in the chair in the photograph.

W I N G   C H A I R

The special feature of this chair is that the wing and arm are joined to form a continuous shape. The fabric pieces for the wing and the arm are shaped and machine stitched together before they are

tacked onto the chair. Refer to the basic instructions on pages 34 to 36 to upholster the rest of the chair. The arms and wings are padded in the usual way.

of the wing, clipping the fabric as you tack to ease it around the curve.

3 Cut two rectangles of fabric for the outer wing and arm allowing 2 in (5 cm) to turn under. Pin and machine stitch together as in step 2 but no shaping is needed in this seam.

4 Tack on the outer wing and arm in the following order. Keeping the seam straight, tack the top of the arm at the front edge, then stretch the fabric slightly and tack the seam of the wing and arm on around the back of the chair. Tack the rest of the top edge of the arm in place, then the lower edge. Tack the top of the wing, then the side back. Finally tack on the front edge of the wing, cutting it like the inner wing to ease it around the curve.

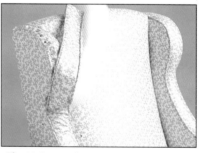

1 Measure the widest points of both the inner wing and the arm in both directions. Add 2 in (5 cm) to turn under. Cut two rectangles of top cover fabric to these measurements.

2 Lay the arm fabric in place and cut a curved line following the join between the wing and the arm to accommodate the padding. Mark this line on the chair. Pin this curved edge to the straight lower edge of the wing fabric, right sides together, and machine stitch. Tack the seam in place at the front over the mark on the chair.

Push the fabric into the gap at the sides of the back until you can feel the wood rails of the top of the back and the upper and lower arm rails. Mark these points and bring the fabric to the front again. Check the vertical grain of the fabric down the wing and arm, then cut the fabric to fit around the rails.

Push the flaps through to the back and tack them down. Tack the fabric under the rail at the base of the arm then under the top rail of the arm. Pull the fabric up toward the top of the wing and tack it down. Tack around the front

5 Make a self-piped gusset to run down the front of the wing and arm of the chair. Pin this in place with a small pad of cotton batting (wadding) under it. Sew the gusset in place using a 2 in (5 cm) curved needle and strong thread. Put a gimp pin at each side of the bottom edge of the gusset at the front of the chair. Tack down the back edge of the gusset to the back of the chair. The raw edges will be covered by the fabric on the back of the chair when it is attached. Repeat on the opposite wing and arm.

FOUR SOFAS

*Traditionally, the back and seat of this type of Victorian Chesterfield-style sofa
are buttoned but since this does make a rather uncomfortable seat for quite
some time after re-upholstery, the buttoning has been omitted.*

*The scroll arms of this sofa are fairly small and set back to allow more leg
room. The seat cushions are boxed, but the back cushions have gathered
"Turkish" corners, giving a more informal style. The attractive shaping of the
frame along the bottom edge would be lost with the addition of a skirt.*

The basic frame of both the sofas on this page is almost exactly the same – seat depth, seat height, back height, and the rake are identical – only the arm structure has been changed. The large rounded arms make this sofa seem larger although the actual seat space remains the same. Loose back and seat cushions and a deep ruffled (frilled) skirt give the piece a feminine appeal and make it very comfortable.

The back of the sofa is "fixed", i.e. it is completely upholstered and back cushions are not needed. Fixed backs may be firm or soft depending on the construction. They may be sprung (as on page 53) or fully padded over a webbing base using hair or foam and batting (wadding) in layers built up to the required depth. The absence of any type of skirt again emphasizes the lines of the sofa, giving it a masculine styling.

BERGÈRE ARMCHAIR

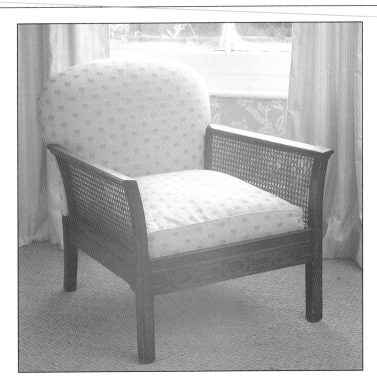

*B*ergère three-piece suites were very popular in the 1920s and 30s. This chair has an upholstered back but there were just as many with caning on the back as well as in the arms. These have a loose back cushion as well as the one forming the seat.

The webbing on the back of the chair in the photograph had stretched at the back, so that the springs were protruding backward, which made the front look flattened.

Materials

webbing
spring twine (laidcord)
cotton batting (wadding)
top cover fabric
$\frac{1}{2}$ in (13 mm) and $\frac{3}{8}$ in (10 mm)
  tacks and tack hammer

1 Strip the webbing off the chair. Renew it and re-sew the springs in place (see page 14).

2 Cover the inside back with batting (wadding), then apply the top cover (see page 35).

3 Next center the top fabric over the outside back, and pin to the frame, turning under the raw edges. To sew in

place, start in the middle of the top of the back, work across the back and down one side, making the stitches as invisible as possible. Repeat on the other side, then tack down the bottom of the back under the bottom rail of the chair.

4 To re-cover the box cushion for the seat, follow the instructions on page 115.

FRENCH SHOW-WOOD CHAIR

*T*his armchair (also known as a "fauteuil") combines comfort with elegance. The style originated in France and dates back to the 18th century. It had a great influence over the development of chair design. The British master

furniture maker, Thomas Chippendale, is known to have imported frames to finish in his workshop.

The upholstery for the chair in the photograph was applied to a new chair frame, so no preparation was necessary.

Materials

webbing
springs
spring twine (laidcord)
heavy-duty and lightweight
  burlap (hessian)
coir fiber
horsehair
cotton batting (wadding)
muslin (calico)
$\frac{1}{2}$ in (13 mm), $\frac{3}{8}$ in (10 mm), and
  $\frac{1}{4}$ in (6 mm) tacks and tack
  hammer
gimp pins
twine
top cover fabric, e.g. silk,
  damask, brocade
black cambric (platform cloth)
braid
buttoning needle
4 in (10 cm) curved needle
liquid fabric cement (glue)

1 Turn the chair upside down and web it on the underside of the frame. Work out the number and position of the strips on the front rail, and mark them. Because the back rail is so much shorter than the front, the webbing may overlap slightly at the back. Tack on the center piece at the front first. Protect the wood at the back with a cloth pad while stretching the webbing. Tack the webbing on. As the frame of the chair is curved at the front, the fold on the next piece of webbing will have to be on the slant so that it can be stretched properly. Use five pieces of webbing from front to back and four pieces across the chair (see page 13).

2 Use eight 4 in (10 cm) springs, two rows of three springs at the front and one row of two springs at the back. Stitch to the webbing (see page 14).

3 Measure the seat from the back of the back rail to the front of the front rail over the springs, then across the widest part of the chair. Add 2$\frac{1}{2}$ in (6 cm) in each direction. Cut a piece of heavy-duty burlap (hessian) to these

measurements. Mark centers of frame and fabric. Match at the back and, using $\frac{1}{2}$ in (13 mm) tacks, tack the burlap (hessian) onto the frame leaving 1$\frac{1}{4}$ in (3 cm) extending beyond the frame.

4 Match the center fronts. Stretch the burlap (hessian) tightly over the springs and tack. Continue tacking along the front to within 4 in (10 cm) of the front corners.

5 To cut the burlap (hessian) around the back of the chair, fold the sides in over the seat and cut from the point of the corner toward the inner side of the back. Pull the fabric around the back and sides and tack it down.

6 To cut around the arms of the chair, fold the burlap (hessian) over onto the seat at the sides. Cut sideways toward the center of the arm, stopping 1 in (2.5 cm) away from it and cut a V shape toward each side of the arm. Pull the fabric around both sides of the arm and tack it down. Finish tacking the rest of the sides and the front. Trim, leaving 1 in (2.5 cm) extending all around the frame. Turn this over and tack it down at 4 in (10 cm) intervals.

7 Spread 26 oz (750 g) of coir fiber evenly on top.

8 Measure from the top of the back rail, over the coir to the front rail, then across the width of the chair at the front (its widest point). Add 2$\frac{1}{2}$ in (6 cm) in each direction and cut a lightweight burlap (hessian) cover to these measurements. Mark centers front and back on the burlap (hessian).

9 Match the back centers. Turn the edge of the fabric in and tack it to the edge of the back rail.

10 Pull the fabric forward and match the center fronts. Tack to the edge of the front rail. Use more coir fiber if the front feels flat.

11 Cut around the back and arms as for steps 5 and 6.

12 Sew an edge roll all around the chair (see page 25). Check that the roll follows the frame exactly. There is a lot of shape in these frames, especially at the center front.

13 Using the buttoning needle and twine, sew down the rest of the stuffing. The stitches should be 4 in (10 cm) long and in rows 4 in (10 cm) apart. Pull the twine taut after each stitch. The seat should look only very slightly domed.

14 Cover the pad with horsehair 1 in (2.5 cm) deep (not compressed). Sew this down loosely in a few places with a 4 in (10 cm) curved needle.

15 Cover the horsehair with batting (wadding). Feather off around the edges by hand, so that the frame is still visible.

16 Measure over the widest part of the chair and cut the muslin (calico) to fit. Mark the center back and front on the fabric and match the back with the back of the chair. Tack it onto the chair. Pull the muslin (calico) forward. Match up the center fronts and tack in place. To tack the rest of the front, pull diagonally toward the front corner with one hand, smoothing the seat forward with the other. Tack to within 4 in (10 cm) of the corner. The grain of the fabric should run in a straight line across the chair.

17 To cut around the arms of the chair, fold the side fabric across the seat. Check that the front edge of the fold and the seat fabric are even. Cut a straight line toward the center of the arm support, stopping 1$\frac{1}{2}$ in (4 cm) away from it. Make a V-shaped cut $\frac{3}{8}$ in (1 cm) long toward the outer edges of the arm. Pull the fabric down either side of the arm and tack in place. Repeat on the other side of the chair.

18 Cut the back corners of the chair as in step 5. Trim the excess muslin (calico) and finish tacking the back and sides.

19 To finish the front corners, bring the side fabric around to the front of the chair and tack it down. Take the front fabric around to the side and tack it down. Trim the excess. Leave the actual corner free for tacks in the top cover.

20 Cut out the top fabric, allowing $\frac{3}{4}$ in (2 cm) extra fabric on all four sides to turn under. Chairs like this one are often upholstered in fine fabrics, such as silks or brocades, which are not strong and fray easily. Having a double thickness of fabric helps to prevent the fabric from pulling away. Check and center any pattern. Apply the fabric as for the muslin (calico) cover, but use gimp pins. As the heads are smaller, they can be placed closer to the edge of the frame and are less likely to show above the braid.

21 To apply the braid, brush glue on the braid, then spread the glue evenly and remove the excess with your finger. Press the braid onto the chair, being careful not to stretch it. Cut it off $\frac{3}{8}$ in (1 cm) beyond the required length. Turn this end in, glue it to itself, and tack it onto the chair with a gimp pin to finish.

THE CHAIR BACK

22 Measure the inside back and add $2\frac{1}{2}$ in (6 cm) in each direction. Cut a rectangle of the top fabric to these measurements, making sure that any pattern is matched with the seat. Do not attempt to cut an oval-shaped piece – the excess can be trimmed after it has been tacked in place. Mark the center top and bottom on the fabric and the chair.

There is only a very narrow area of wood around the frame in which to put the tacks. Take great care not to get the tacks too near the edge of the frame or you will split it. Place the fabric on the inside back of the frame, so that the right side is seen from the back of the chair. Using $\frac{1}{4}$ in (6 mm) tacks, put two tacks at the center bottom through a single thickness of fabric. Pull the fabric upward, stretching it slightly and put two tacks in at the center top.

Continue in this way, putting two or three tacks in at the bottom, then stretching the fabric and putting several in at the top. Keep the grain of the fabric straight. Continue all around the back in this way, constantly checking that the fabric is straight. Trim $\frac{3}{4}$ in (2 cm) beyond the tacks, fold in and tack down every 4 in (10 cm).

23 Tack a layer of heavy-duty burlap (hessian) on top in exactly the same way.

24 Spread a layer of horsehair $\frac{3}{8}$ in (1 cm) thick on the burlap (hessian).

25 Cover the horsehair with a layer of batting (wadding), feathered off by hand (see page 26).

26 Cut a piece of muslin (calico) approximately to the shape of the chair back. Tack in place, turning the edges under.

27 Cut the top cover the same shape as the muslin (calico). Match up the pattern with the center of the seat, if necessary. Using gimp pins, tack the fabric on as for the muslin (calico), turning the edges in.

28 Glue on the braid as for the seat (see step 21).

THE ARMRESTS

29 Some chairs of this design have armrests. To upholster them, tack on a piece of webbing cut slightly smaller than the armrest.

30 Cover the webbing with horsehair $\frac{3}{8}$ in (1 cm) deep, and stitch it to the webbing using the 4 in (10 cm) curved needle and twine.

31 Cover the hair with batting (wadding).

32 Tack a piece of muslin (calico) over this, turning the edges under all around.

33 Tack on the top cover as for the muslin (calico) and attach the braid as for the chair seat.

34 Tack a piece of cambric (platform cloth) to the underside of the chair, cutting the fabric around the corners.

S o f a

The method for upholstering the sofa in the photograph on pages 20–1 is exactly the same, only the dimensions are greater.

BUTTON-BACK CHAIR – METAL FRAME

*D*eep buttoning on chairs and sofas is very much a feature of furniture produced in the Victorian era. Before that, comfort had not been a consideration. However, from the 1830s onward, more and more chairs and sofas were made with deep-sprung seats and softly buttoned backs.

The frame of the seat was always wood, but the back and armrests were often made from strips of iron bolted together and let into the wood of the seat frame. The chair above is an example, as can be seen from the "before" picture on the left.

1 Turn the chair upside down. Support the seat on a work bench. Strip off the cambric (platform cloth) and the webbing and loosen the top cover all around the base of the frame.

2 Cut the springs out of the base of the chair. Test each one by placing it on a flat surface and pushing it down over itself. If it leans over to one side, discard and use a new one.

3 Turn the chair right side up and remove all the layers of the seat. Keep them all at this stage. Leave the back upholstery intact and work on the seat first.

4 Re-web the chair following the basic instructions given on page 13 and the variation for angling the webbing on page 46.

5 Turn the chair over again and place eight 6 in (15 cm) springs on the webbing, two rows of three springs at the front and the other two springs at the back. Point all the joins of wire on the top ring of each spring in the same direction. Draw around the base of each spring, making sure that they are placed well to the front of the frame. Check that the gaps between the individual springs and the rows of springs are equal. Remove the front two rows and start sewing the springs to the webbing (see page 14). Tie the springs in place (see page 15).

6 For the heavy-duty burlap (hessian) cover measure from rail to rail over the springs at the widest part of the frame, and allow an extra 2½ in (6 cm) in each direction. Cut the burlap (hessian) to these measurements. Mark

Materials

webbing
heavy-duty and lightweight
  burlap (hessian)
springs
coir fiber
horsehair
cotton batting (wadding)
muslin (calico)
$\frac{1}{2}$ in (13 mm) and $\frac{3}{8}$ in (10 mm)
  tacks and tack hammer
buttons
twine
top cover fabric*
cambric (platform cloth)
2 in (5 cm) and 4 in (10 cm)
  curved needles
buttoning needle
decorative braid
liquid fabric cement (glue)

*Small prints and tapestry-style
fabrics work well

---

the centers at the front and back of the frame and the fabric, and match up at the back leaving $1\frac{1}{4}$ in (3 cm) of fabric protruding beyond the frame.

There is usually a metal strip attached to the seat frame at the center back. Cut the burlap (hessian) to fit around it by extending the marking for the center back cut until it is 2 in (5 cm) in length. Then cut a V shape as far as the side of the metal strip. Pull the fabric around the strip and tack it down for 4 in (10 cm) either side of the center. Pull the fabric forward over the springs and tack the matched center fronts.

Continue to tack along the front of the frame to within 4 in (10 cm) of the corners. The burlap (hessian) should be tight and will depress the springs further. Cut around any other metal supports as for the center back. Tack down the sides. Allow a turn-over of $1\frac{1}{4}$ in (3 cm) all around the chair and trim off the excess. Turn it over and tack it down. Sew the springs to the burlap (hessian) as described on page 14.

7 Now work on the back of the chair. Take apart the outer back cover and keep it for a pattern. The front top

cover and the back burlap (hessian) are stitched onto the iron frame. Take out all the stitching, cut out the buttons and remove the top cover.

8 Examine the iron frame. Any repairs can be done by a blacksmith. If the frame is rusty, bind it with strips of muslin (calico) 10 in (25 cm) wide.

9 The next stage is to cover the iron frame with burlap (hessian). The back and arms are covered separately and joined after they are sewn in place. Measure the front of the frame and allow and extra 4 in (10 cm) on the length and the width to tuck around the iron bars. Cut a piece of heavy-duty burlap (hessian) to these measurements. Take the burlap (hessian) around under the bottom of the frame and bring the edge $\frac{3}{4}$ in (2 cm) above the frame, so that the frame is wrapped in fabric. Use a backstitch with the 4 in (10 cm) curved needle and twine. Sew as closely as you can to the iron strip. Pull the burlap (hessian) taut as you sew. Pull the fabric up in front of the frame, over the top of it and secure it with pins. Again, keep the fabric taut and sew close to the frame. You may need to clip the burlap (hessian) around the curves of the frame to keep it taut. Sew the

burlap (hessian) on the arm frames in the same way, then join the arms to the back burlap (hessian), again using a backstitch. Trim around the burlap (hessian) to neaten it.

10 Mark the position of the buttons for the chair back on both the front and back of the burlap (hessian). The top row will have five buttons on

it, the second row four buttons, the third row five and the fourth row five. The position of the outer ones will fall where the arm fabric joins that of the chair back.

11 Use the old back pad if it is in good condition. Spread coir fiber to a depth of 1 in (2.5 cm) (not compressed) over the burlap (hessian) on the back and the arms. Sew it down with large stitches all over using the 4 in (10 cm) curved needle. Replace the pad and sew it down. If the pad is not re-usable, cover the back burlap (hessian) with coir fiber at least 3 in (7.5 cm) deep (compressed) and sew down tightly as above.

12 Expose the button mark on the front burlap (hessian) by pushing your finger through the coir fiber and leaving a hole in it.

13 Cover the stuffing with batting (wadding). Expose the button hole positions.

14 Measure the back for the top cover across the widest part of the chair. Allow 4 in (10 cm) to overlap the frame and 1 in (2.5 cm) for each button on the line of measurement. In this case allow an extra 4 in (10 cm) across the chair and the same from top to bottom, making 8 in (20 cm) extra fabric on the length and width. The button sits right down on the back burlap (hessian), pulling the fabric down with it. Cut the fabric.

15 Cut a piece of twine 20 in (0.5 meter) long for each button, then cut the same number of pieces of burlap (hessian) 2 × 1 in (5 × 2.5 cm) which will prevent the twine from tearing the back fabric.

16 Match up the centers at the top and bottom of the frame and top cover. Push the fabric into the middle button hole on the top row. Push the buttoning needle threaded with a piece of twine into this depression and through the burlap (hessian). Pull the needle through. Push it back again through the burlap (hessian) 1 in (2.5 cm) from where it emerged and through the hole in the stuffing. Pull the twine almost through but leave a small loop. Put one of the small pieces of burlap (hessian) in this loop, then pull the twine tight on it. Thread the button onto the twine on the front of the chair, tie a slip knot and pull the twine tight. The button should now go down the hole in the stuffing and sit on the burlap (hessian).

Leave the long ends of twine at the front of the button at this stage. Push the fabric into the two button holes on the next row below. Pleats will radiate from the one you have just put in. Sew these two buttons in place. Check that the center vertical line of the fabric is between them. Next sew on the center button in the third row, then the two buttons radiating from it in the fourth row. Working down the center first makes it easier to keep the fabric straight. Return to the top row and fit in the buttons at the sides. Keep the grain straight. The needle should go in the same horizontal grainline right across the chair.

17 Pin the top cover fabric around the back of the chair. Make pleats from the side and top buttons. Pin in place. Pull the fabric under the bottom rail of the chair. There will be two vertical pleats from the buttons in the fourth row. Pin in place. Using the 4 in (10 cm) curved needle and twine, sew the fabric to the burlap (hessian) all around the back.

18 Measure the arms for the top cover. Add an extra 2 in (5 cm) on the width at the widest part for the join between the arm and the back. There are no pleats as such on the arms.

The buttons act more like retainers to keep everything together. There is no need to make holes in the fiber for the button on the arm. Put the fabric in place on the arm, keeping the grainline vertical. Turn in the seam allowance between arm and back. This will be wider at the bottom as the line of the join slopes slightly inward. Sew a button on the join in line with those on the fourth row of the back. Put another one midway between the previous one and the front end of the arm.

19 Pin and sew the loose edges of fabric around the arm. Pleat the fabric around the front curve. Work on the other arm in the same way.

20 Tighten the slip knot holding each button in place and tie three more ordinary knots to keep the slip knot in place. Cut off the two ends of twine 1 in (2.5 cm) from the knots. Tuck the ends under the button. Repeat this for each button.

THE SEAT

21 Cover the burlap (hessian) with a layer of coir fiber 1 in (2.5 cm) deep (not compressed), then replace the seat pad. Tack down the burlap (hessian) covering it onto the edge of the frame and sew all the way through the pad using the buttoning needle to fix it firmly in place, avoiding the springs and bringing the needle out between the strips of webbing. Use stitches 4 in (10 cm) long and 4 in (10 cm) apart. If you need to make a new seat pad, follow the directions on page 25.

22 Cover the pad with horsehair, 1 in (2.5 cm) in depth (not compressed). Sew down loosely using the 4 in (10 cm) curved needle and twine.

23 Cover the horsehair with a layer of batting (wadding). Feather it off by hand so that the base of the frame is just visible.

24 Measure and cut out the muslin (calico) cover. Tack it in place. Cut around the metal bars of the frame as for the burlap (hessian) covering the springs. To form the front corners, follow the directions on page 26.

25 Measure and cut out the top cover, matching any pattern with that on the back. Tack in place (see page 26).

THE BACK COVER

26 This is made to fit using three separate pieces of fabric joined together before the whole is sewn onto the chair. Measure from the top of the back to the bottom and add 2 in (5 cm). Then take the width measurement from just beyond the point where the back joins the arms and add 2 in (5 cm). Measure from this point to the end of the arms and from the top to the bottom of the arm for the other two pieces. Add 2 in (5 cm) in both directions. Pin the fabric onto the chair all around the frame with the fabric right side out. Pin the seams. These will be on a slant, pointing in toward the center back. Remove the back, re-pin the seams with right sides together and machine stitch the seams. Re-pin it to the back of the chair, right side out, turn under the seam allowance and sew invisibly using the 2 in (5 cm) curved needle and strong thread. Tack the bottom fabric under the chair.

27 Sew or glue the braid over the seam which attaches the fabric to the back of the chair (see page 27).

28 Tack cambric (platform cloth) on the underside of the chair.

B UTTON-B ACK C HAIR – W OOD F RAME

*T*his pretty little chair is very typical of the Victorian period. A lady would sit on it while she stitched her fine needlework.

The secret of good buttoning is to keep the grain of the fabric straight in both directions. The pleats then fall into place.

Materials

webbing
springs
burlap (hessian)
coir fiber
horsehair
cotton batting (wadding)
muslin (calico)
twine
buttons
$\frac{1}{2}$ in (13 mm) and $\frac{3}{8}$ in (10 mm)
  tacks and tack hammer
gimp pins
top cover fabric
decorative braid
cambric (platform cloth)
liquid fabric cement (glue)

1 Follow steps 1 and 2 on page 48, resting the top of the chair back on a piece of foam to protect the carving.

2 Turn the chair right side up, strip off the rest of the seat and remove the fabric on the back of the chair back. Examine the joints of the frame for movement; also check that there is no woodworm. Treat both these things if necessary (see page 12).

3 Loosen the fabric on the front of the chair. Cut the buttons off and remove the top fabric from the chair.

4 On the back of the chair, examine the heavy-duty burlap (hessian) which supports all the upholstery. If it is in good condition, leave it in place. Otherwise strip everything off the back of the chair, replace the burlap (hessian) and put the pad back (see page 49), using tacks to secure the burlap (hessian) instead of sewing it in place.

5 Re-upholster the back of the chair first. Cover the old pad with a layer of batting (wadding). Push your fingers through the new batting (wadding) down to the burlap (hessian) to prepare the button holes. Measure for the top fabric and complete the rest of the preparation following the directions on page 50. Sew on the buttons. The second row of

buttons usually contains the most buttons as it is positioned at the widest part of the chair back.

6 Use gimp pins to tack the top cover down, turning the raw edges under. Make a pleat from each button next to the frame at the sides and top. Make vertical pleats from the bottom row of

buttons. Take the fabric under the back rail, cutting it around any back supports, and tack it onto the back rail. Glue on the braid (see page 27).

7 Re-upholster the seat (see page 50). To finish off the front corners, pull the point of the fabric down over the corner of the chair. Put in a tack on the corner and make pleats from the excess fabric either side of the tack. Bring them toward the corner forming a V shape. Tack down. Trim off the excess fabric around the corner.

8 Measure, cut and shape the top fabric to cover the back of the chair, then fix in place (see page 51).

9 Glue the braid onto the back of the chair and the seat front.

10 Tack cambric (platform cloth) onto the underside of the chair.

CHAISE OTTOMAN

*A*n ottoman is a box with a padded lid and sides. A chaise ottoman has a backrest, so that it is possible to use it as a long chair or bed.

The techniques described here could be used on any box to make it more decorative.

This chaise ottoman was badly stained and the backrest was disproportionately thin. The instructions describe how to remake the backrest, re-line and re-pad the box, replace the springs in the lid and re-cover the whole piece.

Materials

top cover fabric*
lining fabric
muslin (calico)
cotton batting (wadding)
buttons
decorative cord
spring twine (laidcord)
twine
strong thread to match top fabric
webbing
heavy-duty and lightweight
   burlap (hessian)
cambric (platform cloth)
$\frac{1}{2}$ in (13 mm) and $\frac{3}{8}$ in (10 mm)
   tacks and tack hammer
steel wool
buttoning needle
2 in (5 cm) and 4 in (10 cm)
   curved needles
stuffing regulator
back tack strip
chain to hold lid
decorative studs
gimp pins
oil

*cottons and chintzes work well

1 Remove the hinges of the box lid. If they are rusty, clean with steel wool and brush with oil.

2 Strip off all the fabric and upholstery from the box and backrest. Leave the lid until later.

3 Test the springs (see page 28).

4 Re-attach the springs on the backrest by placing the springs on the wood rail as before. Run a piece of webbing over the base of the rings

resting on the wood. Put a tack on each side of the wire at four equally spaced points on each spring. The springs should now be firmly fixed. Stretch a second piece of webbing over the tops of the springs and tack it onto the backrest at each side. Sew the springs to the webbing (see page 14). Attach the next row of springs in the same way.

5 For a heavy-duty burlap (hessian) to cover the springs, measure from the front of the lower rail up and over the springs to the back of the top rail. Add on an extra 2 in (5 cm). Measure over the springs from side to side of the frame. Add on 2 in (5 cm). Cut the burlap (hessian) to these dimensions. Mark centers top and bottom on the frame and the burlap (hessian) and match up. Leave 1 in (2.5 cm) protruding below the lower rail and tack on using $\frac{1}{2}$ in (13 mm) tacks, $1\frac{1}{4}$ in (3 cm) apart. Match up centers from the top rail, stretch the fabric and tack.

Repeat at the sides. Turn over the excess and tack at 4 in (10 cm) intervals. Sew the springs to the fabric (see page 14).

6 Cover the burlap (hessian) with coir fiber to a depth of $2\frac{3}{4}$ in (7 cm) (compressed). Use the buttoning needle and twine and sew the fiber down firmly.

7 For the next layer of lightweight burlap (hessian), measure from the back of the lower rail over the stuffing and up to the back of the upper rail. Add 2 in (5 cm) to turn under. Cut out the burlap (hessian). Use $\frac{3}{8}$ in (10 mm) tacks, $1\frac{1}{4}$ in (3 cm) apart. Turn the

lower edge of the fabric under and tack it to the back of the lower rail. Stretch the fabric up and over the coir and tack it to the back of the front rail, turning under the raw edges. Do the same down each side.

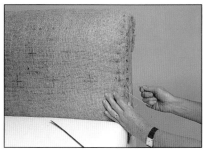

8 Using the 4 in (10 cm) curved needle and twine and a stuffing regulator, sew an edge roll down each side of the backrest (see page 25). Mark button positions.

9 Spread a layer of horsehair over the backrest $\frac{3}{4}$ in (2 cm) deep (not compressed). Stitch loosely to the burlap (hessian) with the curved needle, then cover the hair with batting (wadding), feathered off by hand around the edges. Keep the button positions marked with pins.

10 Measure and cut out the muslin (calico) cover as for the previous layer of burlap (hessian), mark centers and match up. Temporary tack it to the back of the lower rail. Pull the muslin (calico) up and over the upper rail, smoothing it upward as you pull, and temporary tack. Do the same at the sides. Pleat the muslin (calico) around the curved top of the backrest and tack down each pleat. Cut the muslin (calico) around the sides of the lower rail. The backrest should look even and feel firm. Make any adjustments necessary, then hammer in all the tacks.

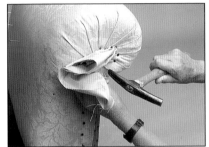

11 Measure the top cover as for the muslin (calico). Cut out the top cover, being careful to center any pattern. Note that whatever you have as the center motif on the backrest must also be in the center of the box lid. Tack the top cover in place as for the muslin (calico). Next mark the position of the buttons with pins. Position the buttons under the headrest in the middle of the backrest. Sew in place (see page 50). Measure and cut the top fabric for the back of the backrest. Back tack in place (see page 36) at the top. Tack the bottom under the box. Tack the sides.

THE LID

12 Strip off the old webbing and cut the strings attaching it to the springs (see page 12). Re-web the lid (see page 13). There is no need to mark out the position of the webbing pieces as they can be placed in the original positions, but avoid using the same tack holes. Sew the springs to the webbing (see page 14).

The rest of the upholstery on the lid was in good condition and did not need attention. However, if more work is needed, follow the directions on page 62.

13 Cover the top of the lid first with a layer of batting (wadding), next with muslin (calico) lining, and finally with the top cover. Make the corners of the lid (see page 26).

THE BOX

14 For the loose lining, take the measurements of the inner sides and the base of the box. Add 1½ in (4 cm) to each measurement for seams at either end. Cut the lining fabric to these measurements. Pin all the sides, right sides together, and stitch the seams. Pin the base to the sides, right sides together, and stitch in place. Fit into the box and tack in place, using ⅜ in (10 mm) tacks 4 in (10 cm) apart on the flat top of each side.

15 Cut batting (wadding) to the measurements of the four outer sides of the box. Secure to the outside with a tack in each corner. Cut pieces of muslin (calico) to the same size but add ¾ in (2 cm) extra in each direction to fold under. Tack the muslin (calico) first under the box, then on the flat top of the sides. Use as few tacks as possible to allow space for the tacks which will secure the top cover. Turn in the muslin (calico) at each corner and secure the side edges with gimp pins.

16 Measure for the top cover, taking the pattern match into account if necessary. Cut each side separately. To position on the box, back tack the long sides on first. Let the fabric drop into the box: the pattern will be upside down with the raw edge on the top of the box. Put a tack at either end of the side. Place the back tack strip on the flat top edge, and, using ⅜ in (10 mm) tacks 1½ in (4 cm) apart, tack it in place. Take the fabric out of the box and over the side. Tack it in place under the base of the box. Repeat with the other three sides. Fold all raw edges in at the corners and sew invisibly (see page 60).

17 Cut two pieces of top fabric to the shape of the sides of the

backrest and two pieces of batting (wadding) 1 in (2.5 cm) smaller all around. Tack on the batting (wadding) in a couple of places. Pin the top cover in place, turning in 1 in (2.5 cm), and sew invisibly using the 2 in (5 cm) curved needle and matching strong thread.

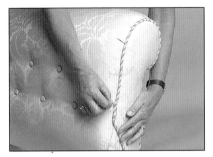

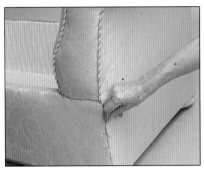

18 Sew decorative cord around the sides of the backrest and top and bottom edges of the box using the same curved needle but passing the needle under one of the strands in the cord, then running it under the fabric, using stitches ¾ in (2 cm) long. Wrap the cord with sticky tape where you need to cut it and cut through the middle of the tape. Tuck the end of the cord out of sight and secure with a gimp pin under the top cover.

19 Replace the hinges. The lid will need some sort of restrainers to prevent it falling backward and pulling the hinges off when open. Use either a piece of chain or hem a strip of the top fabric to make a restrainer. Tack onto the inside of the box with decorative studs at the end opposite the backrest. Tack onto the lid, adjusting the length so that the lid will stay open without being held.

20 Tack cambric (platform cloth) onto the underside of the box.

STOOLS

F ENDER S TOOL

*T*his is a quick project suitable for a beginner. The instructions are adaptable for any stool which has a wood rather than a webbed base to the seat. The stool in the photographs is an antique piece needing new padding and a new cover.

1 Cut the rubberized hair to fit in the base of the seat. Place in position.

2 Cut the batting (wadding) slightly larger than the rubberized hair and lay on top.

3 Cut the muslin (calico) to the same size as the batting (wadding) and place on top. Hold in place with upholstery skewers, so that the fabrics are taut but not too tight.

4 Secure the fabrics with tacks. Start by hammering a tack in the center of each side, then work out to the corners. Keep the corners sharp and neat. Check that the padding is of an

even depth. Re-tack any places that are uneven, then trim away the excess muslin (calico), close to the tacks.

5 Cut the top fabric to the same size as the muslin (calico). Place on top of the stool. Line up the fabric so that the grainline is parallel to the side of the stool. It is important that the edge of the fabric is the same distance from the outside edge of the stool on all four sides. Hold in place with upholstery skewers.

6 Begin by tacking down a short side, leaving the corners free and starting in the center. Tack the opposite short side, then the two longer sides. Finally, trim the corners and tack down.

7 If using cord, hold in place along the edge of the fabric with large pins. Stitch in place using curved needle and strong thread. Make the join near but not on a corner. If using braid,

spread a thin layer of glue on the back of the braid and press in position. Miter the corners.

Materials

rubberized hair
cotton batting (wadding)
muslin (calico)
tack hammer and tacks
craft knife
top cover fabric
cord, gimp, or braid to decorate
curved needle
strong thread
upholstery skewers
scissors*
liquid rubber cement (glue)

*Use an old pair of scissors to cut the hair, as they will blunt quickly.

*O*VER-*S*TUFFED *S*TOOL *W*ITHOUT *S*PRINGS

*T*he upholstery on this stool looked to be in reasonable condition. However, it is always advisable to check all the layers and stages in the upholstery process before simply re-covering. It is not possible to produce a good finished piece if all the layers beneath the top cover are not firm and even. Once this particular stool had been looked over, the webbing was found to be slack (you should not be able to push webbing up and down, it should be absolutely rigid), so the stool was stripped right down to the frame.

1 Strip the stool down to the bare frame. Examine the joints for movement and the frame for any signs of woodworm. Treat both these things if necessary (see page 12).

2 Re-web the upper side of the stool frame (see page 13).

3 Measure, cut, and tack a new burlap (hessian) cover over the webbing (see pages 24–5).

4 Replace the old seat pad. If it is flattened in the center, add extra hair under the pad to even it up. Tack the pad down onto the edge of the frame using ³⁄₈ in (10 mm) tacks, 1¼ in (3 cm)

apart. If you have to make a new pad, follow the directions on page 25, steps 6–8.

5 Use a buttoning needle and twine to sew the pad down. Stitch through all the layers of the seat, with stitches that are 4 in (10 cm) long in rows 4 in (10 cm) apart.

6 Spread a layer of horsehair to a depth of ³⁄₄ in (2 cm), not compressed, over the seat pad. This will fill in the indentations made in the pad by the previous stitching. Sew it down loosely onto the pad in just a few places

using the 4 in (10 cm) curved needle and twine. Cover the hair with a layer of batting (wadding) and feather the edges by hand parallel to the top of the sides of the frame. An edge cut with scissors gives a hard line, which will show through the top cover.

7 For the muslin (calico) cover, measure from under the frame and over the stuffing in both directions. Cut the muslin (calico) to these measurements. Mark the centers on the short sides of the muslin (calico) and the frame. Use ³⁄₈ in (10 mm) tacks to secure the center of one of the short sides, then work outward to the corners. Stretch the muslin (calico) over to the other short side, smoothing it as you stretch, and tack in the center first, then along the rest of the side. Tack the long sides in the same way. All tacks should be driven in only halfway at this stage as you will need to adjust them.

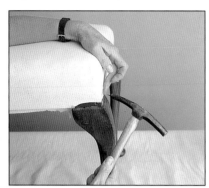

8 Cut the muslin (calico) to go around the leg, and tack just off the corners to leave the actual corner free for the tacks which will be used on the top cover. Check that the cover is smooth and firm, then hammer in all tacks.

9 Measure and cut the top cover as for the muslin (calico), then tack down in a similar manner, taking care that any geometrical pattern of the fabric is lined up with the edges of the stool, and any motif is centered.

Cut the fabric at the start of the legs on the shorter sides. Bring the fabric around onto the longer side over the top of the leg, tucking in the raw edge as it passes over the top of the leg and tacking it down.

10 Form the corners by folding the fabric in to get the vertical lines, then cut away the excess fabric from inside the fold.

11 Stitch down the corners using a 2 in (5 cm) curved needle and strong matching thread. Secure the thread at the top of the fold. Run the needle ¼ in (6 mm) along inside the fold, then the same distance through the

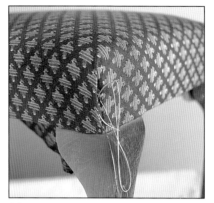

fabric it rests on. Continue in this way to the bottom of the fold and finish off. It should not be possible to see these stitches. Hammer in a matching gimp pin at the bottom of the fold for extra strength.

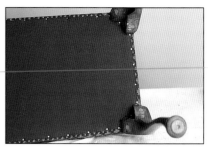

12 Tack cambric (platform cloth) onto the base of the stool, cutting it to fit around the legs.

Materials

webbing
burlap (hessian)
horsehair
twine
cotton batting (wadding)
muslin (calico)
½ in (13 mm) and ⅜ in (10 mm) tacks and tack hammer
top cover fabric
strong thread to match top fabric
gimp pins to match top fabric
buttoning needle
2 in (5 cm) and 4 in (10 cm) curved needles
black cambric (platform cloth)

STOOL WITH FEATHER CUSHION

*T*his stool needed considerable reconstruction of the upholstery before being fitted with a re-covered cushion. The cushion is attached to the stool by an integral cover. The instructions below are for a plain cushion but it can also be buttoned, if liked, as in the photograph.

Materials

webbing
spring twine (laidcord)
heavy-duty burlap (hessian)
horsehair
twine
cotton batting (wadding)
1 in (25 mm), ½ in (13 mm), and
  ⅜ in (10 mm) tacks and tack
  hammer
gimp pins
black cambric (platform cloth)
top cover fabric
springs (if required)
4 in (10 cm) curved needle
buttoning needle

1 Strip the stool down to the bare frame (see page 12). Keep the seat pad and the cushion.

2 Test the joints of the frame for movement and repair if necessary (see page 12).

3 Test each spring by putting it on a flat surface and pushing it down over itself. If it leans over to one side, discard and use a new one.

4 Re-web the underside of the frame (see page 13).

5 Arrange the springs on the webbing. Draw around the bases of the springs. Remove all but the row you are working on and sew in place (see page 14).

6 Tie down the springs to each other and the frame (see page 15).

7 Measure from the outer side of the top of the frame over the springs to the opposite side of the frame. Add 2½ in (6 cm) in each direction. Cut a piece of heavy-duty burlap (hessian) to these measurements. Mark the centers on the front and the back of fabric and frame and match them up. With 1¼ in (3 cm) of fabric extending at the back of the frame, tack down the burlap (hessian) using ½ in (13 mm) tacks, 1¼ in (3 cm) apart.

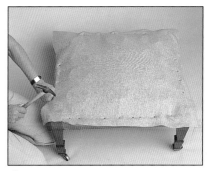

8 Match the centers at the front, pull the fabric tightly toward the front and tack it down as at the back. Repeat

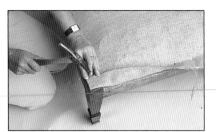

the process at the sides. The fabric should feel very tight, with the springs compressed slightly more than they were after tying. Turn over the raw edges of the burlap (hessian) and tack them down at 4 in (10 cm) intervals.

9 Sew in the springs. Make sure that the heads of the springs, visible through the fabric, are evenly spaced. Use a 4 in (10 cm) curved needle and twine (see page 14).

10 Spread 7 oz (200 g) of horsehair on top and replace the horsehair pad – the extra horsehair will fill out the depression made in the pad over the years. Use more if necessary.

11 Using ⅜ in (10 mm) tacks, tack the pad onto the front edge of the frame.

12 Using the buttoning needle and twine, sew the pad down onto the springs. Go through the pad using stitches 4 in (10 cm) long in rows 4 in (10 cm) apart, pulling the string taut after each stitch.

13 Cover the pad with a layer of batting (wadding) and feather off around the edges by hand.

14 From the top cover fabric you will need a stool cover (one piece) and a separate box cushion (top, bottom, and edge strip). For the stool cover, measure the width and length from under the wood rail on one side of the stool, over the top and down the opposite rail. Add enough turning allowance for the fabric to fit comfortably underneath. Cut the box cushion to the dimensions of the top of the stool plus seam allowances.

15 Mark the center point of the stool and the halfway points along each side. Repeat for the bottom of the box cushion. Make up the box cushion following the instructions on page 115 to end step 9, but with the zipper set against the piping rather than in the center of the edge strip. (The stool will be moved around, therefore will be seen from all angles, so the zipper should be as invisible as possible.) You may prefer to omit the zipper and slipstitch the opening together. In this case, make the opening only from corner to corner.

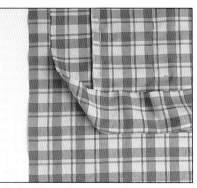

16 Place the part-made cushion over the stool cover, right sides together, matching the center points. Make sure the cushion is exactly centered by matching the halfway

points and measuring from the piping to the raw edge of the stool cover all around. Pin in place making a square of pins approximately 5 in (12 cm) in from the sides of the cushion cover. Machine stitch along this pinned line. Turn the stool cover piece inside the "box" and stitch the cushion cover top to the edge strip, right sides together. Turn the cover right way out and with it the stool cover. Press.

17 Mark the centers on each side of the stool. Place the cushion and stool cover fabric over the stool, matching centers. Tack the centers of the cover under the stool. Tack down each side, working out from the center.

18 Cut the top fabric around the front legs at the side. Bring the fabric around to the front, fold in the raw edge and tack it down. Cut vertically to the top of the stool beyond the tacks. Cut around the front leg as at the side, fold under the raw edge and make a vertical fold on the corner. Fold the fabric back on itself and cut off the excess fabric. Turn the fabric back and secure the corner with a gimp pin. Sew invisibly from the top of the corner down to the gimp pin. Repeat on the other front corner, then on the back corners.

19 Insert the cushion into the case. Cover the base with cambric (platform cloth), using ⅜ in (10 mm) tacks, 2 in (5 cm) apart.

FABRIC-COVERED TABLE OR STOOL

*T*hese instructions can be used to make a fabric-covered piece of furniture to serve as a coffee table, side table, or a bedside table, or to use as an occasional or end-of-bed stool. If the table will be used for drinks, a glass top cut to the exact size can be fitted inside the piping line to protect the top fabric. The wooden framework can be either made up or purchased ready-made in medium density fiberboard (MDF).

Make up the table or stool in a plain color with contrast piping. In a starkly decorated room, fabric-covered tables in complementary colors can add a softer touch. Piping can be stitched to the top only, or to the top and the bottom of the side panel, and may be self-colored or in a harmonizing or contrasting color.

Materials

sarille or cotton interlining
top fabric
curved needle
piping covered in top or
   contrasting fabric
liquid fabric cement (glue) and
   1 in (2.5 cm) brush
small piece of felt or baize
metal studs (for base of each leg)
piping cord

1 Measure the top of the table and add ¾ in (2 cm) seam allowance all around. Measure the legs around the widest part and the length from the bottom of the side panel. Add ¾ in (2 cm) seam allowance all around. Measure the side panel all around and add 4 in (10 cm) to the depth plus ¾ in (2 cm) to the length. Draw a cutting layout on graph paper to work out the total amount of fabric required.

2 Cut the pieces of fabric in both interlining and top fabric, making sure that any patterns in the latter are centered on the table top, and evenly placed on the legs and side panel.

3 Working on one leg at a time, spread glue thinly on each side.

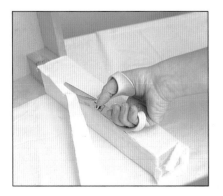

4 Press the interlining leg piece onto the glued area, smoothing out any wrinkles and keeping the raw edges on the inside corner of the leg. Cut away so the raw edges of the fabric meet on the corner, with no overlaps. Repeat with the other three legs.

5 Glue the side panel in place all around, so that the top raw edge of the interlining is even with the top of the table. Mark around each leg and cut away the excess fabric, so that the interlinings butt up. Fold the center "flaps" under and glue to the underside of the table.

6 Cut the table top piece of interlining so that it is just ¹⁄₁₂ in (2 mm) larger than the wood. Spread the glue over the top and lay the interlining on it. Fold over each side and pinch the excess together with the side panel to make a slightly rounded edge all around the top.

7 Check for any bubbles in the interlining. If there are any, pull back the interlining and refit. The whole table must be smooth at this point or the top cover will not lie flat.

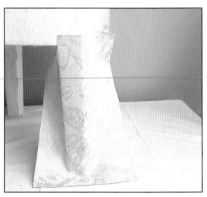

8 Take one of the top fabric leg pieces and lightly fold in half lengthwise. Pin this fold along the length of the outside edge of the leg, so that it extends slightly at the top and bottom of the leg. Pull the fabric around the leg on both sides and pin to the next corners. Cut into the seam allowance where the leg joins the side panel to allow the fabric to bend around the leg.

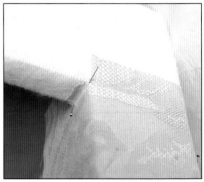

9 Cut a small flap under the side, so that the raw edge will be covered with the side panel piece later.

10 Cut away the leg fabric on the inner corner, so that one side is flush with the leg and the other overlaps by $\frac{5}{8}$ in (1.5 cm). Glue along the inside edge of the leg so that the overlap will wrap over and secure. Lightly glue the inside of the overlap and press in position on the leg. The raw edge should be held by the glue, so that the fabric at the corner will not fray. Repeat with the other three legs.

11 At the bottom of each leg, cut away the excess fabric to $\frac{3}{4}$ in (2 cm). Clip into the corners and fold the fabric onto the wood to neaten the bottom of each leg. Cover with a small square of felt and tap on a metal stud if the table will be moved often.

12 Make up the top as follows. Machine stitch the piping all around the edge of the table top piece on the seam allowance (see page 18).

Join the short ends of the side panel to make a continuous circle. Mark this piece with the measurements of the four sides, placing the seam at one of the

corners. Align each of these sections to the four sections of the top piece, with right sides together. Pin and machine stitch as close to the piping as possible. Turn right side out and check that the piping stitching is not visible. If it is, stitch again inside the previous stitching lines. Trim the seam and press. Add piping to the bottom edge of the side panel at this stage, if desired.

13 Pull the top onto the table, making sure that the seam allowance faces in the same direction all around. Pin to the interlining along the top edge and at the corners to anchor in place.

Mark the top lines of all four legs and clip the fabric so it can be turned under at these points.

14 Fold under the excess fabric at the top of each leg and pin. Fold the center "flaps" between the legs under the table top and glue to secure. Pull these firmly to make the top taut.

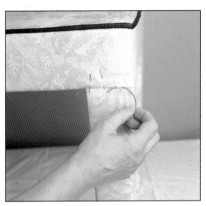

Finish off the joins by stitching small stitches with a curved needle. Finish the inside of the table by covering with a piece of felt or spare fabric.

Fabric-covered Stool

To make into a stool, make up a box cushion using the dimensions of the table top with a thickness of 2 to $2\frac{1}{2}$ in (5–6 cm). The pad can be filled with any feather or feather/down mixture, or a hair or foam pad can be used (see page 122) if you prefer a flatter look. Follow the instructions for the box cushion cover on page 115.

HASSOCK

*T*his footstool was probably made before or just after World War II, since the inside stuffing is straw. Straw was often used as an alternative to horsehair in utility furniture. Occasionally shredded paper was used as a substitute for hair. There is no need to replace such a stuffing, but it will probably need to be added to or at least to be lifted and aerated to improve the shape after many years of use.

The central core is coiled springs stitched together and webbed all around. The webbing will probably also need replacing.

Materials

top fabric
lightweight and heavy-duty
 burlap (hessian)
upholstery thread
piping cord
decorative cord
webbing
stuffing regulator
horsehair or coir fiber
curved needle

1 Remove the outer cover and use to calculate the amount of top fabric needed. Remove any old lining fabric and cut replacement pieces. Make sure that all old stitching, pieces of old fabric, canvas, etc. are removed.

2 Check the condition of the springs and stuffing. Replace the webbing strips and re-stitch the springs if necessary (see page 14). Lift the stuffing with the regulator to restore the original shaping. Add some hair or coir fiber to any places which are very worn down, to give an even line and shape. Make up a lightweight burlap (hessian) cover to fit tightly over the stuffing.

3 Cut out a circle from the top fabric to fit over the top, adding $\frac{5}{8}$ in (1.5 cm) seam allowance. Cut a circle of heavy-duty burlap (hessian) the same size for the bottom. Make up enough piping to go around each circle. Measure the circumference and the depth of the side. Allow one-and-a-half to two times the circumference and cut a piece of top fabric to these measurements plus seam allowances. Machine stitch the two short ends together to make a continuous circle .

4 Pin the piping all around both circles on the right sides. Clip into the seam allowance to allow the piping to lie flat. Machine stitch securely.

5 Divide the circumference measurement by 10. Mark the outside edge of the top circle into 10 equal sections with pins. Measure the

circumference of the fabric ring. Divide this figure by 10 and mark into sections along the top edge as before. Stitch a gathering thread $\frac{3}{4}$ in (2 cm) below the top edge. Pin the marked sections of the fabric ring to the corresponding marks on the top circle, right sides together. Working section by section, gather the side piece to fit the top so that the gathers are even all around. Pin from the gathered side. Machine stitch from the same side. Remove all pins, turn over and machine stitch again around the circle as close to the piping as possible. Keep the gathered fabric straight underneath as you are working.

6 Position this piece onto the stool top, right side up so that the top is flat and the gathered side is folded up on top of the stool out of the way. Using a large needle and strong thread, stitch the seam allowance all around into the burlap (hessian) cover. This will prevent the top from sliding and keep the surface flat.

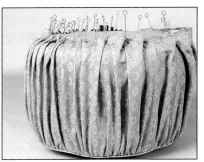

7 Pull the gathered fabric down over the side and secure to the lower edge with pins. Work all around, keeping the grain straight and the gathering even. Stitch to the burlap (hessian) to secure.

8 Press the circle for the base of the stool so that the piping and seam allowance face inward. Trim away excess fabric as necessary.

9 Place this circle over the bottom of the stool and center. Using a curved needle and strong thread, stitch behind the piping into the top fabric, picking up and securing the gathers.

10 Tie a piece of decorative rope around the middle and add knots, tassels, etc., to suit your room.

BOXES AND BASKETS

LINING A VICTORIAN BOX

*B*ecause the inside surface of the box will vary in size, you will need to cut each piece of cardboard as required, so keep the cutting equipment nearby. It is important to measure and cut extremely accurately, as the pieces will not fit together if there is even a slight discrepancy in the measurements. The fabric should be lightweight, such as silk or satin.

Materials

top fabric
cardboard (thick card)
lightweight polyester batting
  (wadding) to fit the insides of the
  lid and base
craft knife
cutting board
1 in (2.5 cm) wide sticky tape
white (paper-to-fabric) glue
point turner (plioir)

Order of working

Lid: front and back pieces;
      side pieces;
      inside top
Box: front and back pieces;
      side pieces;
      base.

1 Working in the above order, first measure inside the lid for the front and back pieces. Measure the depth in several places and in at least two places for the length, especially on an old box which will be worn around the sides.

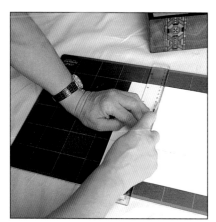

2 Transfer these measurements onto the cardboard, and cut out using a flat ruler and craft knife. Mark the side of the cardboard which will be against the wood, so that the correct side is covered with fabric.

3 Place the fabric right side up on the worktable. Position the cardboard over, wrong side up. Cut around the cardboard, allowing ⅝ in (1.5 cm) to turn under on each side.

4 Spread a thin layer of glue on the unmarked side of the cardboard. With the fabric on the table, right side down, position the cardboard, so that the margins are equal all around. Press down. Turn over and quickly smooth out any bubbles with the flat of your hand.

5 Cut across each corner of the fabric to within ⅛ in (3 mm) of the cardboard corner. Spread a thin layer of glue ⅝ in (1.5 cm) wide along one long side of the cardboard. Fold the fabric over, pressing the point turner against the inside of the cardboard to give a clean, tight edge, then flatten the fabric onto the cardboard. Press the edge of the point turner against the short edges of the cardboard into the corners to flatten the fabric against the cardboard. Spread the glue as before along one short side. Fold over the fabric as before, using the point turner to make a neat corner.

6 Repeat with the other long side, then the other short side. Always work around each piece of cardboard one side after the other, rather than working on the long sides and then the short sides.

7 Spread a thin layer of glue on the back of the cardboard and on the side of the box lid. Press the cardboard against the box lid and hold in place for a few seconds until the glue has fused.

8 Repeat with the other long side. Measure the short sides between the new fabric sides and repeat as above.

9 To make the lid top, cut two pieces of cardboard, one to the exact measurements of the inside of the box between the new sides and one piece ¹⁄₁₆ in (2 mm) wider.

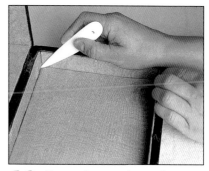

10 Fasten the two pieces of cardboard together with tape along the long sides. Cut one piece of the batting (wadding) to fit inside this "folder." Tape the other three sides together, enclosing the batting (wadding) to make a pad. Spread a thin layer of glue on the top of this pad and press down onto the fabric. Turn over and quickly smooth away any bubbles with the flat of your hand. Cut across the corners to within ⅛ in (3 mm) of the card and fold in the sides and corners as before. Spread the glue on the inside of the box and on the cardboard. Position the pad inside the box lid. Press into the sides with the point turner and press the lid base down firmly with your hands.

11 The lid is now complete. Repeat these steps to line the inside.

BLANKET CHEST

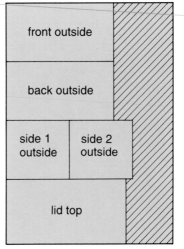

top fabric

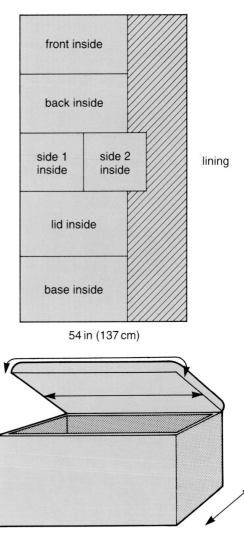

lining

54 in (137 cm)

*B*lanket chests can be put to many more uses than the traditional one of storing blankets. Nowadays we do not need to store large quantities of extra blankets during the summer: our centrally heated houses and duvets have combined to make bedding less of a problem between seasons. Covered boxes, however, can be used to store a multitude of different possessions, including toys, school books, board games, magazines, and out-of-season clothes.

The lid can be slightly padded and this storage facility can then double as a bedside table, a coffee table, or, more fully padded, as extra seating.
Measure accurately:
a) the four internal sides and base
b) the four external sides
c) the inside lid
d) the lid top

Allow $\frac{3}{4}$ in (2 cm) seam allowance all around and plan a cutting layout to fit the chosen fabric. The diagram opposite shows cutting layouts for the piece in the photograph, using 54 in (137 cm) wide fabric.

cutting layout – blanket chest

Materials

top fabric
lining
rubberized hair or foam pad cut
  to fit the top plus ⅜ in (1 cm) all
  around
cotton or polyester batting
  (wadding) to cover lid and sides
cotton fabric to cover base
muslin (calico) to cover pad and
  sides
staple gun and staples
tack hammer and tacks
chain to hold lid
2 brass studs to fit chain
metal feet or casters
liquid fabric cement (glue)
back tack strip
covered piping (optional)
curved needle

1 Unscrew the hinges and remove
the lid from the base. Cut out the
lining pieces for the internal sides and
base. Machine stitch each side to the
corresponding edge of the base along
the seamline. Machine stitch the sides
together from the base to the top,
stopping ¾ in (2 cm) from the top. Press
the seams flat. Place inside the box and
fit to the top of the sides with staples,
cutting and folding under the raw edges
around the hinge positions.

If using piping, staple in place along
the top outside edge of the box.

2 Dab the top of the lid with glue.
Place the pad on top so that the
sides are overhanging by ⅜ in (1 cm) all

around. Place the batting (wadding)
over the pad, cutting or tearing away
around the edge to fit.

3 Place the muslin (calico) on top
and tack to the underside of the lid
with temporary tacks. Continue to tack
at intervals around the inside of the lid,
pulling the fabric as tight as possible
without destroying the shape of the top.
Fold under the corners, clipping away
enough fabric for the corner to fold
neatly. Hammer in the tacks firmly
when you are satisfied with the result.

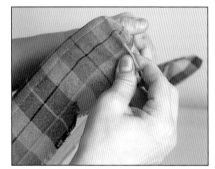

Trim away any excess fabric. Place the
top fabric on top, centering any pattern.
Fit as for the muslin (calico).

4 Cut the lining for the underside of
the lid, fold and press under the
seam allowance, then tack or staple in
place, covering all raw edges and tacks.

5 Cut the four external side pieces
from the top fabric. Staple in place
to each side of the box with back tack,
overlapping at each corner.

6 Stitch the side seams using a
curved needle and matching
thread.

7 Tack the lower edge to the
underside of the box. Cut a piece
of cotton to fit the base. Turn under ⅜ in
(1 cm) all around and press, then tack or
staple in place on the underside to
cover all raw edges and tacks.

8 Refit the hinges, making allowance
for the extra bulk of fabric.

9 Fit a length of chain to the lid and
to the inside of the box, long
enough for the lid to stay open by itself.
Attach the ends with brass studs. Fit the
metal feet or casters.

OTTOMANS

*O*ttomans are wood boxes traditionally used for storing either blankets and bedcovers during the summer season or general bedlinen for spare beds all year round.

When you strip an ottoman down, you might well find that it has been made from fruit or even ammunition boxes, due to a shortage of raw materials at the time it was constructed. These boxes are usually strong enough to take re-covering or can easily be reinforced at each corner on the inside if necessary.

Materials

top fabric
lining for box inside
interlining to cover box
back tack strip
staple gun and staples or tack
  hammer and tacks
decorative cord or rope
lightweight upholstery gimp
curved needle
chain to hold lid
2 brass studs to fit chain

1 Strip off the outer fabric and the inside lining. There may be several layers of fabric which have been put on top of each other over a period of time. They should all be removed together with any tacks or staples. Remove the hinge and reserve. Repair any woodwork at this stage. Measure the size of the pieces which will be needed for the new cover and lining, inside and outside, allowing ¾ in (2 cm) extra on each measurement for the top cover to turn under . Plan the cutting layout and calculate the amount of fabric needed.

2 Cut out enough interlining to fit exactly around the external sides of the box and tack or staple lightly in position, butting up the joins and keeping the joining line straight. Cut a rectangle of top fabric to fit exactly around the box, plus ¾ in (2 cm) for seam allowances on the short sides and the same amount to turn under on the long sides.

3 To make up the lining, cut the four interior side pieces and the box base. Machine stitch each of the side pieces to the respective side of the base piece. Machine stitch the four pieces together from the base of each of the corners to the top.

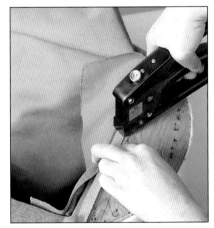

4 Fit the lining into the box, with the seams on the inside. Tack or staple the inside top edge to the top edge of the box. Trim away excess fabric at corners to reduce the bulk to a minimum. Cut away and turn in the raw edges around the hinge. If the design of the box has flat surfaces at the top, cut strips of the lining fabric the width of the flat area and machine stitch the pieces around the top of the opening. Tack or staple to the sides of the box. Press all seams flat from the back and front.

5 Keeping the top edge straight, pin the outside cover to the top edge of the box. Overlap the sides. Fold under the raw edge. Pin and stitch in place using a curved needle and matching thread. Trim the excess at the top edge to $\frac{3}{8}$ in (1 cm). Fold under the raw edges to align with the top of the box. Pin and stitch in place.

6 Keeping the fabric straight, pin to the box along the lower edge. Turn the box upside down and fold the fabric to the underside. Tack or staple in place all around.

For a circular or oval box, clip the fabric at frequent intervals up to the edge of the box, so that the fabric will lie flat. If the fabric is thick, cut out notches and butt the edges to form a neat edge.

For a square or rectangular box, cut into the corners and fold to form neat right angles. Cut away any excess fabric which will cause bulk, as the box will not sit on the floor evenly if there is too much fabric at the corners.

7 To cover the lid, cut out a piece of top fabric to the required dimensions and center over the ottoman top. Pin all around at roughly 4 in (10 cm) intervals to secure. Pin all around the bottom edge, pleating or

gathering the fabric as necessary. If the shaping of the lid is very pronounced, you will need to cut out notches so the fabric can be pulled around neatly with minimum bulk.

8 Turn the lid over and staple or tack the fabric to the underside as for the base, pulling to keep the top smooth and making small pleats where necessary.

9 Cut out a piece of lining the same size as the lid. Pin to the underside of the lid, covering all raw edges. Fold under $\frac{3}{8}$ in (1 cm) all around and tack or staple neatly along the edges. Use colored tacks or cover visible staples with narrow gimp. Trim with decorative fringe or braid.

10 Refit the other side of the hinge to the lid. Tack a piece of chain to the ottoman and to the lid with brass studs, so that the lid will stay open without straining the hinge.

If you would prefer to have a fabric restrainer, cut a strip of fabric $1\frac{1}{4}$ in (3 cm) wide and 6–8 in (15–20 cm) long, fold lengthwise into thirds and machine stitch. Tack the raw edges between the lining cover and box on the side and lid.

Ottoman Variations _____
Ottomans and other storage boxes come in all shapes and sizes. Some are padded on the top with foam, some are flat, and some have sprung lids. The sides may be plain or shaped, and the whole frame may be upholstered or the sides may be set onto a wood base.

Whatever the style of box you wish to upholster, you will find the relevant instructions by following one or a combination of the projects described in this book. The fender stool (page 58) shows how to cover a rubberized hair lid; the chaise ottoman (page 53) a webbed and sprung lid; the over-stuffed stool (page 59) a lid with a horsehair pad; the blanket chest (page 72) a simple wood box; the firescreen (page 105) and inset screen (page 106) a wood frame with fabric panels.

HATBOX

*H*atboxes have been revived as decorative accessories during the past few years. As well as the traditional shapes for men's and women's hats, there are boxes in all shapes and sizes (from 3 in/7.5 cm round to 28 in/70 cm hexagon) available for purchase, covered or uncovered.

If you buy a new box it will be clean and ready to cover. An old box will need to have its outer cover removed completely before you start. You cannot cover over the existing fabric whatever its condition, because the added thickness will prevent the lid from closing.

Materials

top fabric
lining fabric
white (paper-to-fabric) glue and
  ⅝ in (1.5 cm) brush
ribbon or other trimming
fine interlining (if the lid closure
  space allows)

1 Measure: (a) the circumference and the height of the box, (b) the circumference and the height of the lid.
The pieces you will need in top fabric are: outside box; outside lid; outside lid top, and in lining fabric are: inside box; inside box base; inside lid top; inside lid. The outside and inside lid can be cut in one piece if you are using the same fabric for the top and the lining. Plan the layout of the pieces on top fabric and lining.

2 If the lid is not too tight against the box, cut a piece of interlining the exact circumference and depth of the outside box and outside lid. Cut pieces to fit the inside and outside lid tops.

3 Spread a thin layer of glue on the box and carefully position the interlining. Use the flat of your hand to remove any bubbles immediately. Repeat for remaining three pieces.

4 Cut the piece of top fabric for the outside box, allowing ¾ in (2 cm) seam allowance all around. Machine stitch the two short sides, right sides together, along the seamline to make a continuous circle. Slip the fabric over the box and secure at top and bottom with pins at eight points around the box. Make sure that the grain of the fabric is straight. Turn the box upside down. Spread a thin layer of glue ⅝ in (1.5 cm) wide on the base around the outside edges. Clip into the seam allowance of the fabric at intervals to allow it to lie flat and press onto the glued line one piece at a time, working around the box. Spread a similar amount of glue around the inside top edge of the box. Fold the fabric over the top edge into the box,

pressing with your fingers to eliminate any bubbles. Make sure the fabric is pulled tight to give a clean fold and a neat edge.

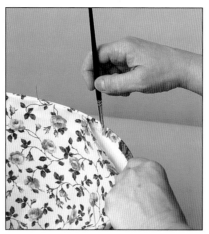

5 Cut the lining piece for the internal sides and machine stitch together to make a continuous circle. Fold ¾ in (2 cm) at the top edge to the wrong side. Along the bottom edge make ⅝ in (1.5 cm) clips at ¾ in (2 cm) intervals. Spread another thin layer of glue around the edge of the base. With the wrong sides of the fabric against the box wall, position the lining so that the top folded edge runs exactly along the inside top of the box and the clipped edge lies on the box base. Overlap the clipped fabric pieces on the box base and finger press onto the glue line.

6 Measure the diameter of the inside of the box accurately. Cut a circle of lining fabric to this diameter. Spread a thin layer of glue all over the box base. Position the base fabric. Finger press firmly to the sides. There should not be any frayed edges, but if there are, wait until the glue has dried, then trim them with very sharp scissors. (If you do this before the glue is dry, you could easily pull the circle out of shape.)

7 From the top fabric, cut the outside lid top with ⅝ in (1.5 cm) extra to turn under. Center it on the lid and pin in place to secure. Spread a thin layer of glue ⅜ in (1 cm) wide all around the outside top of the lid side. Press the edges of the lid piece down onto this, clipping all around to help the fabric lie flat. Trim as necessary.

8 Cut a piece of top fabric the circumference of the lid side and the depth of the outside and inside lid side with ⅝ in (1.5 cm) seam allowance all around. Seam the short sides. Press under the seam allowance along the top edge, then slip over the box. Pin the foldline to the edge of the box. Spread glue inside the box lid along the bottom of the sides. Fold the lower edge of the top fabric in and press into place.

9 Hand stitch the side to the top with tiny stitches.

10 Cut and fit the inside lid in the same way as for the base.

PICNIC BASKET

*P*icnic baskets and hampers are very much part of summertime in the country; if not in the fields or at the seaside, then at one of the open-air displays or concerts, held in the grounds of a substantial country house, which are becoming more and more popular. The best china, crystal, silverware, and champagne accompany simple fare of bread, cheese, and summer fruits, or a well-prepared game pie and chutney.

Even though the opportunities for actually setting the "table" and eating leisurely outside may be limited by unreliable weather, an enjoyable picnic may still be had in winter in a sheltered spot, as long as everyone is warmly clothed.

The pleasure of eating seems to be enhanced not only by the fresh air but also by the peculiar ritual of unpacking a well-stocked hamper.

The picnic box lining serves both to hold utensils in their separate compartments and to keep out sand, grass, etc. The cutting layout opposite shows the pieces for the basket in the photograph.

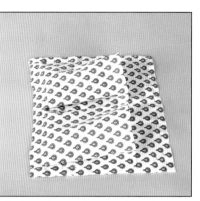

Materials

fabric
matching grosgrain ribbon, ¾ in
(2 cm) wide for edging, and ⅜ in
(1 cm) wide for ties
lightweight polyester batting
(wadding) to cover top and
sides

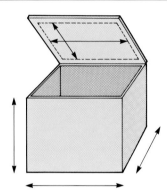

1 Measure the height and width of
the four internal sides of the
basket, the inside lid, and the base,
keeping in mind that the lid lining
should sit inside the basket sides when
the lid is down. Add ⅝ in (1.5 cm) all
around for seam allowances.

2 Cut two lid pieces to the
dimensions measured, including
the ⅝ in (1.5 cm) seam allowance all
around. Cut two strips of fabric 7 in
(18 cm) wide and the length of the
shorter side of the lid. Make a double

hem ⅜ in (1 cm) wide on the right hand
side of one piece and the left hand side
of the other. Machine stitch.

3 Place one of the lid pieces right
side up on the worktable. Pin these
two strips to either side, lining up the
raw edges and with the hemmed edges
toward the center. Mark horizontal
stitching lines from top to bottom of the
strips at ¾ in (2 cm) intervals,
measuring from the seamline. These
spaces will contain silverware (cutlery),
so check that yours will fit into these
spaces. Adjust the spacings to suit your
own implements if necessary, then
machine stitch through both layers.
Fasten the ends securely. (If required,
flaps to cover the ends of the pockets
can be made and attached at this point.)

4 Place the lining piece exactly over
this piece, right sides together, and
a layer of batting (wadding) on top. Pin
securely and machine stitch around
three sides. Turn right side out. Press
seams flat. Press the seam allowance
under along the unstitched side and
slipstitch together to close. Stitch ties to
the corners and across the pad as
necessary to fit it to the lid of the
hamper.

5 Cut the four side pieces and the
base pieces, allowing ⅝ in (1.5 cm)
seam allowance all around. Cut the
lining to the same measurements.

6 To make pockets for the sides, cut
out two pieces of fabric to two-
thirds the basket height and the length
of the short side plus enough to go
around the items intended to fit the
spaces (on average 8 in/20 cm extra).
Pin to the bottom and sides of the side
pieces of the lining, folding the excess
into pleats at the bottom.

7 Make up the outside and the lining
separately, leaving one of the sides
open on the base. Press the seams.
Place right sides together. Insert ties at
each corner and at roughly 6 in (15 cm)
intervals along the top edges. Machine
stitch around the top edges. Press this
seam. Turn the lining right side out
through the unstitched side. Press all
the seams again, especially the top fold.
Press under the seam allowances of the
unstitched side and slipstitch together.

8 Tie the inside and the lid pads to
the wicker basket.

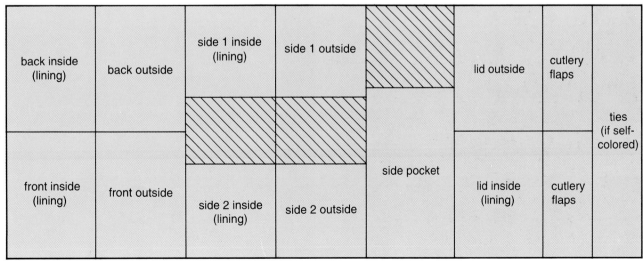

54 in (137 cm)	back inside (lining)	back outside	side 1 inside (lining)	side 1 outside		lid outside	cutlery flaps	ties (if self-colored)
	front inside (lining)	front outside	side 2 inside (lining)	side 2 outside	side pocket	lid inside (lining)	cutlery flaps	

cutting layout – picnic basket

HEADBOARDS

*H*EADBOARDS

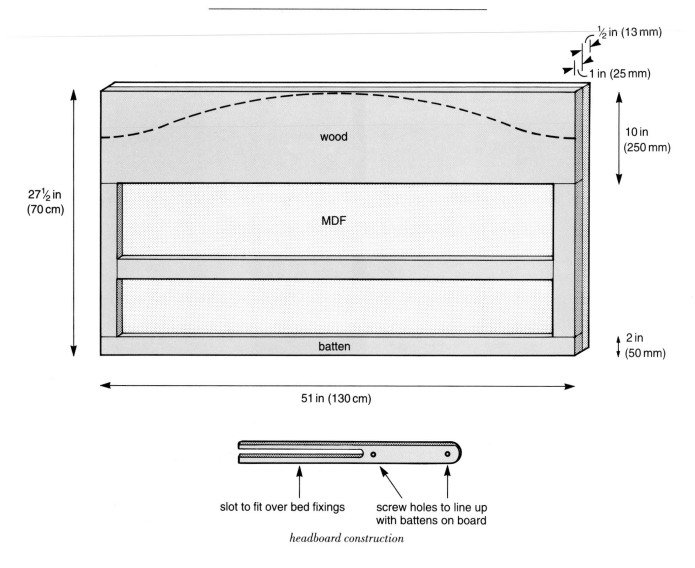

½ in (13 mm)

1 in (25 mm)

10 in (250 mm)

27½ in (70 cm)

wood

MDF

batten

2 in (50 mm)

51 in (130 cm)

slot to fit over bed fixings   screw holes to line up with battens on board

headboard construction

*B*y using modern materials – foam and a staple gun – a wide variety of padded headboards can be made to match the fabric of your bed covers or the decor of your room. The base of the headboard is made from medium density fiberboard (MDF), reinforced at the top with beechwood, and with two struts across the back to support the legs, as shown above. There are many different ways of covering the board, with a gathered or pleated border, with a contrasting fabric border, and with decorative cord or piping.

The instructions in this chapter also include a headboard padded with a duvet and two alternative slip covers (loose covers).

To Construct the Base Board

1 Cut ½ in (13 mm) medium density fiberboard (MDF) to the width and height of the finished headboard.
2 Glue and screw wood and battens, as shown, to the back.
3 Make a template of the chosen shape at the top of the headboard. (A selection of six different shapes for the top is given on page 85.) Cut the top, shaping around your template.
4 Make legs to fit to the bed or attach mirror plates to fix to the wall.

SIMPLE UPHOLSTERED HEADBOARD

*T*his is the most straightforward headboard to make as it can involve as few as three pieces: front, back, and piping. Since there is no real interest in the construction, the fabric and the shape of the top are important to give character.

Interesting shapes can be made, including very elaborate twists and curls, since the fabric is simply fitted to the board, then anchored into place with tacks or staples, without the complication of removing it for stitching. The fabric can, therefore, be pulled and cut into many more shapes, nooks, and crannies than a slipcover (loose cover) would be able to accommodate. Six different shapes are shown on page 85.

Materials

headboard frame
1½ in (40 mm) thick fire-retardant foam
lightweight polyester batting (wadding) to cover
muslin (calico) to cover back and front, approximately 1¾ yds (1.5 m) for single; 3½ yds (3 m) for king-sized headboard

top fabric, approximately 1¾ yds (1.5 m) for single; 2¾ yds (2.5 m) for king-sized headboard
lining for the back: fine burlap (hessian), heavy muslin (calico) or black cotton
piping cord to fit around sides and top
liquid rubber cement (glue)

staple gun with ¼ in (6 mm) and ⅜ in (10 mm) staples
back tack strip
curved needle and matching thread
craft knife

---

1 Draw a line on the headboard 6¼ in (16 cm) above and parallel to the bottom edge. Cut the foam to fit the front of the headboard up to the marked line. Plan the cutting position for the top fabric, so that any pattern is centered, to fit over the foam. Allow 1¼ in (3 cm) all around for seams, and join sections to fit if necessary. Cut the muslin (calico) to the same measurements.

2 Spread a thin layer of cement (glue) on the top of the headboard. Place the foam slab on top, exactly lining up the top and side edges.

3 Holding the staple gun ⅛ in (3 mm) from the edge and using ¼ in (6 mm) staples, staple around the four sides. The staples should be close together and the foam will fold back on itself to make a rolled edge.

4 Cover the foam with batting (wadding), teasing it around the sides, so that it covers the foam well but leaves a soft edge. If the rolled edge is uneven, cut it back slightly with a craft knife, or roll the edge of the batting (wadding) to fill in.

5 Place the muslin (calico) on top of the batting (wadding) with the lengthwise grain of the fabric exactly aligned with the vertical center lines of the headboard. Pin all around the sides to anchor, then staple the muslin (calico) along the base line of the foam. On the other three sides, staple to the back of the board, approximately ¾ in (2 cm) inside the edge. Trim to the outside line of the board.

6 Place a piece of muslin (calico) over the back of the board. Cut to shape to fit the outside edges of the headboard. Fold under ⅝ in (1.5 cm) all around and staple in place, leaving a neat edge.

7 Fold the top fabric in half lengthwise along the lengthwise grain, right sides together, and crease the fold lightly. Using a tape measure, find the center vertical line of the headboard and mark with pins. Place the fabric on the headboard, with the fold of the fabric against the center line. Lifting the top piece of the folded fabric, anchor the under piece to the headboard by carefully transferring the pins from the center line to the inside of the foldline, so that the fabric is secured, with the grain of the fabric and the pattern absolutely straight. Even a small discrepancy at this stage will be obvious when the headboard is in place.

8 Starting at the center top, fold the raw edge of the fabric over to the back and staple in place. Clip as near to the board edge as necessary to enable the fabric to lie flat over the edge and on the front, especially around the shaping. Next fold the fabric at the sides to the back of the board and staple in place. If the corners are sharp, fold the fabric under as a dart; if rounded, ease the corners into shape. Staple along the bottom edge of the fabric, close to the foam.

9 Cut a piece of top fabric to the width of the board plus 4 in (10 cm) and to the depth of the uncovered area plus 4 in (10 cm). Place on the bottom edge of the covered foam, right sides together and raw edges matching. Back tack and staple. Smooth the fabric down over the uncovered area and staple to the back of the board, folding in the corners.

10 Make up enough piping to fit across the top and down the sides (see page 18).

11 Cut a piece of muslin (calico) to the exact shape of the headboard plus ¾ in (2 cm) seam allowance all around. Cut two strips of the top fabric 5 in (13 cm) wide to fit along both sides and one strip 12 in (30 cm) wide to fit across the top. Pin and stitch these pieces to the muslin (calico) lining. Cut around the top edge of the top fabric to match the shape of the muslin (calico).

12 Pin the piping along the sides and top of the headboard and back tack in place, so that the piping makes a neat edge. Clip into the seam allowance as necessary to allow the piping to lie flat on any curves and clip a V shape into the corners.

13 Hold the back piece of fabric against the front of the headboard and back tack to the piping seamline across the top, holding the edge of the back tack against the seamline.

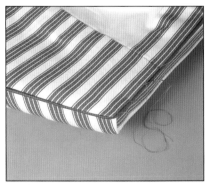

14 Fold the back piece over and secure to the lower edge at intervals to hold. Fold under the raw edges at each side and stitch to the piping using a curved needle and matching thread. Neaten the lower edge and staple or tack in place.

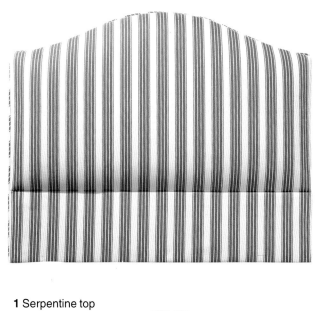

4 D-shaped

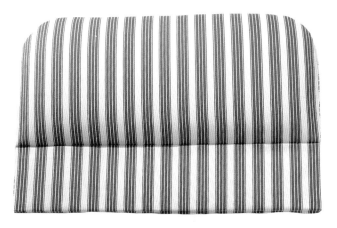

1 Serpentine top

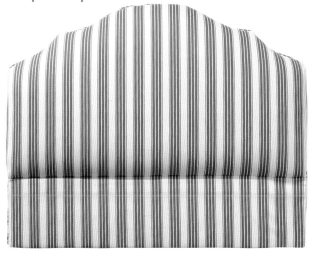

2 Serpentine top with cut corner

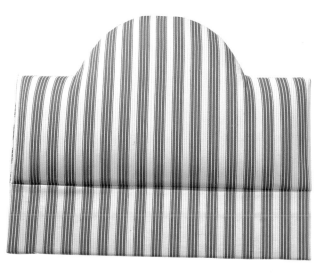

5 Half-moon shaped

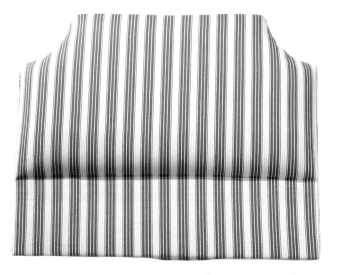

3 Straight top with cut corner

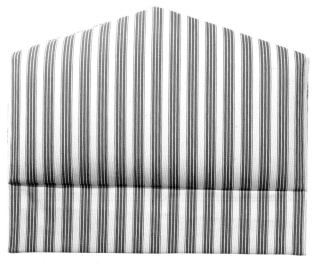

6 Pointed top

P ADDED H EADBOARD

W i t h   G a t h e r e d   B o r d e r

*T*he following instructions are for a headboard with a gathered border and piping in a solid color taken from the top fabric. The cutting layouts below are for twin (single) and double beds. When estimating the amount of fabric needed, add enough extra fabric in the same or contrast color to make $8\frac{1}{4}$ yds (7.5 m) piping for a twin (single) bed or $11\frac{1}{2}$ yds (10.5 m) for a double.

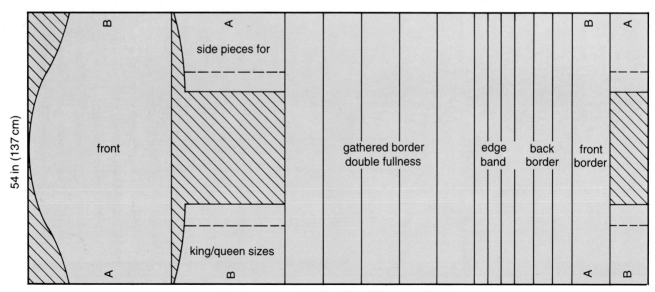

cutting layout – padded headboard for a double bed

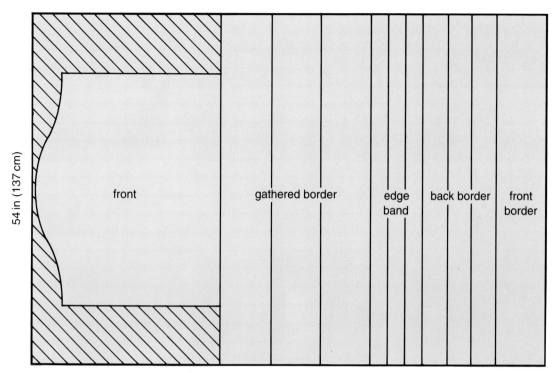

cutting layout – padded headboard for a twin (single) bed

54 in (137 cm)

front | gathered border | edge band | back border | front border

Materials

headboard frame and two legs
  (see page 82)
1½ in (40 mm) thick fire-retardant
  foam
craft knife
liquid rubber cement (glue)
staple gun and staples
lightweight polyester batting
  (wadding)
muslin (calico)
medium-weight cotton for top
  fabric
corded piping (see page 18)*
back tack strip
burlap (hessian)

*see above for quantity

1 Measure the depth of the mattress. Mark this depth on the headboard (usually 6–8 in/15–20 cm). Mark the center top and bottom of the board. Cut the foam to cover the board down to the mattress line, leaving the top unshaped. Place the foam on the worktable. Place the headboard on top, lining up the

sides and center top. Draw a pencil line around the wood on the foam. Cut the foam to this line using a sharp knife.

2 Pencil a 4 in (10 cm) border on the sides and top of the board. Around the shaped top, mark the distance with a series of dots and draw a line to join the dots.

3 Mark a 4 in (10 cm) border on the foam in the same way. Cut out the border *in one piece* and set aside.

4 Spread a thin layer of cement (glue) over the center panel of the board and press the foam in position.

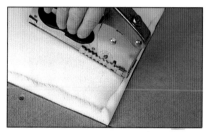

5 Holding the staple gun ⅛ in (3 mm) from the edge of the foam, staple on all four sides. The foam edge should spring back to form a roll over the staples. Place the staples close together to make a smooth edge.

6 Cut a piece of batting (wadding) slightly larger than the foam, and place over the foam. Cut a piece of muslin (calico) the same size as the batting (wadding) and place on top. Staple to the line marked on the board with a staple every 2–3 in (5–8 cm). Do not put the staples too close together as you will be adding another set in between.

7 Mark the center vertical line of the board with a row of pins through the foam. Lay the top fabric over the board and make sure any pattern detail is in the best position. Cut out as planned. Fold lightly in half, right sides together, and line up the fold along the pinned line. Pin the fabric to the foam along the inside of the fold. Keep checking the placement of the pattern, as it is very important that the grain of the fabric remains vertical.

8 Staple at the center top, center bottom and center sides to stretch the fabric evenly, then staple all around. You will not be able to see the drawn line, so hold a ruler in one hand and the stapler in the other to keep the line of staples at an even distance from the edge of the board. Pull out the fullness of fabric to give a smooth finish at the corners, so that the fabric is not pleated.

9 Measure the border at its widest point, i.e. diagonally at the corner. Measure around the sides and top of the center panel. Cut a strip of fabric to this width plus 2 in (5 cm) and to two-and-a-half times this length. Cut piping to the measured length (see page 18). Gather the fabric strip on one long edge and draw up to fit the piping. Machine stitch close to the piping.

10 Place the gathered strip on the fabric-covered board, right sides together and raw edges matching. Push the piping line down onto the staple

line. Place back tack strip against the piping, and staple to the board through the back tack, close to the edge. At the corners, cut the back tack square, ease the fabric around the corner, and clip into the piping seam allowance, so that the piping is tight and makes a good square edge. On curved sections, cut the back tack into small strips. It is not flexible enough to bend.

11 Replace the foam border. Glue in position and staple as before, around all sides and across the ends.

12 On the edges, pull the gathered fabric taut so that the gathers are straight and even. Staple into the edge of the board. At the corners, pull the fabric diagonally and staple. Trim away excess fabric.

13 Cut a piece of fabric to the width of the board plus 4 in (10 cm) and to the depth of the uncovered area plus 4 in (10 cm). Place on the bottom edge of the central panel, right sides together and raw edges matching. Back tack and staple. Smooth fabric down over the uncovered area and staple to back of board, folding in the corners.

14 To make the edge band (gusset), measure all around the board and add 2½ in (6 cm). Measure the width of the headboard frame and add seam allowances to both sides. Cut a strip of fabric to these measurements. Add piping to both sides of the strip, stitching along the seamlines. The space between the two rows of piping should equal the headboard frame width. Cut another strip 4 in (10 cm) wide and machine stitch to the piping on the back of the edge band, right sides together, raw edges matching.

15 Place the band on the board, wrong side up, so that the piping opposite the attached strip is just on the front of the board. Lay on back tack, and staple.

16 Cut a strip of batting (wadding) to the width and length of the board thickness. Place the batting (wadding) along the board under the edge band. Press the seams of the band to the center, pull the strip attached to the band to the back and staple. At the bottom of each side, trim back the piping cord inside the casing and turn under the casing. Trim excess fabric.

17 To finish the back, cut a piece of burlap (hessian) to the dimensions of the board. Place over the back of the board. Turn under a seam allowance at the center top and bottom. Staple. Using a sewing gauge or ruler to keep a constant measurement, turn under the seam allowance all around the burlap (hessian), and staple in position.

DUVET HEADBOARD COVER

I was first attracted to this style of headboard by a picture in a magazine, where it was used on a modern bed, matched with large pillows, all in strong, contemporary colors. I have since used it in many situations where an informal setting is required, such as a child's room, or a cottage bedroom, or where it is needed as a foil to an otherwise straight-edged design. It is less expensive than a fully upholstered headboard and is easily laundered.

Materials

1 duvet*
1 piece of block board or ½ in (13 mm) plywood, the width of the bed × 16–25 in (40–65 cm) high
top fabric
lining fabric to cover the board
2 or 4 toggles (optional)
2 or 4 large buttons to match the top fabric (optional)
thin cord or buttonhole thread (optional)
4–8 × ½ in (13 mm) strips of fabric tape for bottom ties, approximately 10 in (25 cm) each
8 × 1 in (2.5 cm) strips of fabric tape for side ties, approximately 16 in (40 cm) each
drill and bit to make a hole in the board (optional)
liquid rubber cement (glue)

*inexpensive fiber filling, single or double depending on size of bed

1 You will need to cover the board with fabric. This will be visible only at either side, so plain cotton or lining fabric can be used for the greater part, with a panel of the top fabric stitched at either side. This covering may be either glued onto the board or made up as a slipcover.

2 Cut the duvet to the width of the headboard plus 4 in (10 cm) and double the depth of the headboard plus 4 in (10 cm) (measure from the bottom front to the bottom back of the headboard), and finish the raw edges.

3 Cut two pieces of the top fabric for the front and back of the duvet cover, to these measurements *plus* a seam allowance of 2½ in (6 cm) on the length and 1½ in (4 cm) on the width.
If more than one width of fabric is needed, join pieces to either side of the center width at this stage, being careful to match the pattern on the seams.

4 Place the front piece of the top fabric on the worktable, right side up. Mark the center of each long side. Divide the distance between the center and the bottom edge into 3 to 4 equal parts and mark. Pin 2 to 3 ties on these marks. (The number of ties needed varies with the height of the headboard.) Repeat from the center to the top edge.

5 Place the back piece of top fabric over the top, right sides together. Pin the two pieces together along the two long sides, securing the ties, and across the top on the seamline ¾ in (2 cm) in from the edges. Place a pin on the bottom edge 8–16 in (20–40 cm) in from each side (depending on the size of the cover). Pin on the seamline 1½ in (4 cm) from the edge, from the sides up to these two pins.

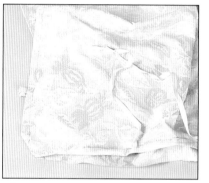

6 Machine stitch around pinned line. Press. Trim the four corners. Turn under a ¾ in (2 cm) double hem along the open bottom edge of each side and pin. Pin ½ in (13 mm) ties at 10–12 in (25–30 cm) intervals along both sides of the bottom edge, exactly opposite each other. Tuck the raw edges of the tapes into the fold, and turn the tape over, so that it is pinned in place falling toward the bottom of the headboard cover.

7 Machine stitch the folded edge and tapes in position. Trim the seams and press flat from the wrong side. Turn the cover right side out. Stuff the duvet into the cover, making sure that it extends all the way into the corners.

8 Tie the bottom ties together. Slip the cover over the board and tie the side ties. It can be left at this point or it can be buttoned to the headboard.

9 Mark the position for the buttons on front and back of the duvet. Untie and remove the cover. Using a large drill bit on a hand or electric drill, make 1 or 2 holes in the board to coincide with the button positions.

10 Thread a large needle with thin cord or buttonhole thread and pass through the duvet cover from the front to the back at one of the marked button positions. Tie the thread around a toggle at the back. Bring the thread back through the cover to the front and through the button. Tie the two ends of the thread together and pull tightly enough that the button and toggle pull into the duvet cover and make it look "puffed". Repeat this process on the front and back of the duvet at each button position.

11 Fold the cover over the board again. Push the front toggle through the hole in the headboard and leave at the back. Push the back toggle through the hole and leave at the front. Repeat with the other set of buttons and toggles. The toggles should now be pulling quite tightly. Tie the side ties into bows.

12 To remove for washing, undo the toggles from the headboard. Cut the threads holding the toggle and button together. Replace after laundering.

SIMPLE LOOSE-COVERED HEADBOARD WITH TIES

*L*oose headboard covers have the distinct advantage over upholstered ones of being easy to remove for laundering or dry cleaning. Two covers can be made up using the same pattern either in the same fabric or in a different design. The covers can then be changed with the seasons.

Materials

fabric: approximately 2 yds (2 m) for a single; $3\frac{1}{2}$ yds (3.5 m) for a double headboard

piping cord: approximately 3 yds (3 m) for a single; 4 yds (4 m) for a double headboard

contrast fabric for ties and piping if desired, $\frac{1}{2}$–1 yd (0.5–1 m)

pieces of $\frac{1}{2}$ in (13 mm) wide fabric tapes, 12 in (30 cm) long, to tie underneath: 6 pieces for single; 10 for double headboard

yardstick (meter ruler)

1 Measure the height and width of the headboard. Add $2\frac{1}{2}$ in (6 cm) to the width measurement and $3\frac{1}{2}$ in (9 cm) to the height to allow for hem. Using the yardstick (meter ruler) and pins, mark two rectangles to these measurements on the fabric for the front and back pieces. If the fabric is patterned, position the front piece carefully, so that the main pattern will be positioned slightly toward the top of the headboard. (The lower 6–7 in (15–18 cm) will be below the mattress and the next 8–12 in (20–30 cm) will be hidden by pillows.) Cut out these two pieces. Place a line of pins down

91

through the center front and back of the headboard.

2 Lightly fold the two pieces of fabric in half lengthwise, right sides together, along the grain of the fabric. Lay the front piece over the headboard with the center fold along the marked center line. Lifting the top piece of the folded fabric, anchor the underpiece to the headboard by carefully transferring the pins from the headboard to the foldline of the fabric. It is very important that the fabric is positioned on the straight of the grain. Even a small discrepancy at this stage will be obvious when the headboard is in place. Anchor the whole piece to the headboard at 4 in (10 cm) intervals all the way around. Position and anchor the back piece to the back of the headboard in the same way.

3 Starting at the center top, and working from the back of the headboard, pin the front and back pieces together along the top and sides. This pinned line will be the stitching line, so the positioning of the pins is crucial for a good fit. The pins must lie in a straight line, nose to tail, along the back edge of the headboard. You will need to hold the fabric firmly between finger and thumb and ease in the fullness from the front piece around any top shaping. Pin the excess fabric at the corner into a dart.

4 Trim away the excess fabric all around to leave a ¾ in (2 cm) seam allowance. At the corners, clip into the seam allowance from the sides. Fold the dart inside, toward the top, and, using thread to match the background of the fabric, stitch along this dart with small ladder stitches. Fasten off with a triple stitch on the seamline.

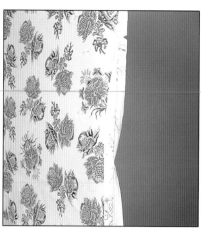

5 Mark the tie positions on the front and back with tailor tacks in a contrasting thread. The top tie should be approximately 4 in (10 cm) down from the corner, and there should be 3–6 per side depending on the height of the headboard.

6 Clip notches into both layers of the seam allowance at 6–8 in (15–20 cm) intervals all around the sides and top to provide matching points for accurate stitching. Fold a ¾ in (2 cm) double hem along the lower edge of the board.

7 Remove the cover. Make up enough piping to go around the sides and top of the headboard and along both sides again (see page 18). Remove pins from the front and back pieces. Pin the piping to the back piece along the seamlines. Clip into the piping stitching line at the corner and fold the piping firmly to make a sharp corner (see page 18). Machine stitch in place, stitching as close to the piping as possible.

8 Pin the front to the back, matching the notches and easing fabric where necessary. Pin close to and along the piping line, and also at right angles to the piping where necessary to ensure that gathers are eased in. The pins which are across the piping can remain in position during machine stitching to prevent the fabric from moving. Start and finish pinning just above the top marked tie positions on either side. Machine stitch the front to the back along the pinned line.

9 Pin piping along the sides of the front piece, from the join with the back piece to the bottom, and machine stitch in place.

10 To make the ties for the sides, cut the required number of strips of the top fabric 2½ in (6 cm) wide and 16 in (41 cm) long. Make into ties as described on page 17.

11 Pin the ties to the front and back piping on both sides, with the centers of the ties on the marked points.

12 Make a placket and facings for each side. To do this, cut two strips of fabric 4 in (10 cm) wide and two pieces 2 in (5 cm) wide times the length from the top of the opening to the hem. Pin the 2 in (5 cm) strips, wrong sides up, to the side opening on the back, securing the ties at the same time. Machine stitch. Repeat to stitch the 4 in (10 cm) strips to the front.

13 Fold the 2 in (5 cm) strips over to enclose the seam. Press and slipstitch to the back cover. Fold the 4 in (10 cm) strips in twice to enclose the seam and slipstitch to the seamline. Machine stitch these two strips together inside at the top join at either side.

14 Pin tape strips at three or four places along the hemline on opposite sides to tie the cover under the headboard. Machine stitch the hem, securing the tapes at the same time.

15 Slip the cover over the headboard and tie the ties on the sides and bottom.

LOOSE-COVERED HEADBOARD WITH EDGE STRIP

*I*f the headboard frame is made up following the instructions given, an edge strip will be needed around the outside edge, as the covered board and frame will be $1\frac{1}{2}$–2 in (4–5 cm) deep. The edge strip prevents the fabric from being pulled too tightly around the shaping, which would distort the shape, and allows the piping to be brought to the

outside line of shaping to become an important detail. The cutting layouts overleaf are for twin (single) and double beds. When estimating the total amount of fabric needed, add enough extra in the same or contrast color to make $5\frac{1}{2}$ yds (5 m) piping for a twin (single) headboard and $7\frac{3}{4}$ yds (7 m) for a double.

SINGLE

54 in (137 cm)

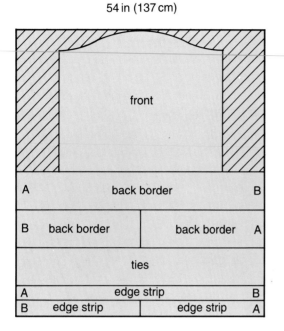

DOUBLE

54 in (137 cm)

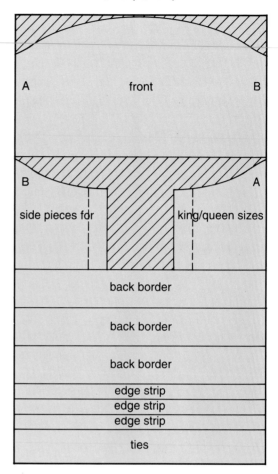

cutting layouts – loose-covered headboard with edge strip

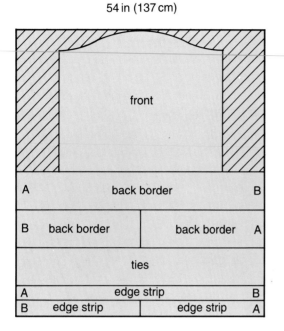 *(single layout labels: front; A — back border — B; B — back border / back border — A; ties; A — edge strip — B; B — edge strip / edge strip — A)*

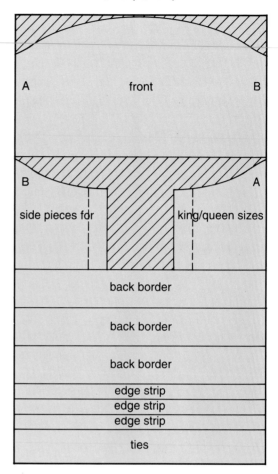 *(double layout labels: A — front — B; B — (side pieces for / king/queen sizes) — A; back border; back border; back border; edge strip; edge strip; edge strip; ties)*

Materials

headboard upholstered with
   muslin (calico)*
top fabric: approximately 1¾ yds
   (1.5 m) for single; 2¾ yds
   (2.5 m) for king-size bed
lining to cover back
covered piping or flanged cord†
pieces of ½ in (13 mm) fabric
   tape, 12 in (30 cm) long, to tie
   underneath: 6 for single and 10
   for king-size

*see page 84, steps 1 to 6
†see step 4

1 Measure the height and width of the headboard. Add 2½ in (6 cm) to the width measurement and 3½ in (9 cm) to the height to allow for hem. With the top fabric flat on the worktable, right side up, mark the front piece to these measurements with pins to determine the best position for cutting. Remember that any large motifs should be positioned nearer the top of the headboard, so that they can be seen once the mattress and pillows have taken up their space.

2 A border of the top fabric is also needed for the top and sides of the back. (The rest is out of sight and can, therefore, be cut from lining fabric.)

3 For the edge strip, measure the distance around the top and both

sides and the width of the upholstered headboard. Add ¾ in (2 cm) to both long sides for seam allowances. Plan a piece to these measurements. If you are using striped fabric, it will be much easier to make an edge strip which has the stripe following the perimeter of the headboard than to match the stripes at the top edge. Patterned fabric should follow through – up the headboard and over the top.

4 Decide whether you want to use self piping, contrasting piping, or flanged cord to finish the top edges, and plan the materials accordingly. You will need enough to fit twice around the top and sides of the headboard.

5 Cut out these pieces. Piece (join) where necessary.

6 Cut the lining piece to the height and width of the board minus the top fabric borders, plus seam allowance as above.

7 Make up the back piece by machine stitching the borders of top fabric to the top and sides of the lining fabric.

8 Mark the center vertical line on the front and back of the headboard with a row of pins. Fold the front piece in half lengthwise, right sides together. Lightly finger press the center fold. Place the fabric onto the board with the foldline along the line of pins. Lift the top piece of fabric and anchor the underpiece to the muslin (calico) covering the board by carefully transferring the pins from the board to the inside of the foldline on the top fabric. It is very important that the fabric should remain centered and the grainline absolutely straight. Even a small discrepancy at this stage will be obvious when the headboard is in place. Anchor the top fabric to the muslin (calico) all around the edge at 4–6 in (10–15 cm) intervals. Repeat with the back piece.

9 Fit the edge piece all around the headboard, right side up, anchoring it in place by pinning into the sides of the cover, across the edge strip at right angles.

10 Starting at the center top and working out to the corners, hold the fabric pieces firmly between fingers and thumb and pin the front to the edge strip. Ease any fullness in the front piece around any curves. The pin lines

will be the stitching lines, so make sure that the seam allowance on the edge strip is even all the way around and that the pins lie straight and close together.

11 At the corners, stop pinning at the seam allowance. Clip into the edge strip right up to the seam allowance and open out, so that the strip fits around the headboard corner at a right angle. Pin the pieces together along both sides. Repeat with the back piece.

12 Trim away the excess fabric on the front and back pieces, cutting to the seam allowance. Cut notches into both layers of fabric at 6–8 in (15–20 cm) intervals. These will be matched up when the fabrics are repositioned for stitching, so must be accurate.

13 Fold up the hemline to line up with the lower edge of the headboard. Remove all anchor pins. Remove the cover from the headboard.

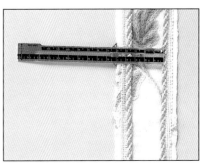

14 Remove the pins holding the front piece to the front of the edge strip. Turn the cover inside out. Pin piping or flanged cord along the seamline the length of the edge strip and machine stitch in place. Matching all notches, fit the front piece to the edge strip, right sides together, easing in fullness as necessary. With edge strip uppermost, pin along the seamline. Also pin at right angles across the piping every 2–2½ in (5–6 cm). These pins can remain in place while stitching to prevent the fabrics from moving.

15 Machine stitch from the edge strip side as near to the piping as possible. Make sure that you stitch inside the previous line where the piping was stitched to the strip, or these stitches will show from the front. Trim the seam allowances.

16 Remove the pins holding the back edge strip to the back piece and machine stitch together, including the piping as before.

17 Slip the cover back over the headboard to check that the seamlines are even and the cover fits well. Finger press the seam allowances toward the center of the edge strip. Mark the positions for the ties on the bottom edges, avoiding the bed legs.

18 Neaten seams. Turn up the front and back pieces along the seamline, inserting ties into the hemline at marked positions. At the sides, pull the piping cord from inside the casing. Cut away the cord level with the hemline (see page 19). Fold the empty casing neatly into the hemlines. Machine stitch the hemline, double stitching over the ties.

ROOM TREATMENTS

TYPES OF SCREEN

Traditional jointed frames can be expensive, due to the labor cost of the carpentry; cheaper versions from shaped pieces of board make adequate substitutes. Screens are used to cover unattractive items – from a television set to a radiator – or to prevent drafts and may therefore be placed in an area which can be very cold in the middle of the night and very warm when the heat is turned on, so the frame and the chosen fabric must be able to adapt to these extremes.

TRADITIONAL FRAME SCREENS

The wood used should be a well-seasoned hardwood which will not warp in temperature changes.

Each screen panel may be from 10 in (25 cm) to 24 in (60 cm) wide and from 30 in (75 cm) to $8\frac{1}{4}$ ft (2.5 m) high, and a screen may consist of two, three, or four panels hinged together. The thickness of the wood will vary from 1 to 2 in (25 to 50 mm) depending on the size of the individual panels. The hinges should be mortised (housed) into the wood to allow enough space for the fabric to return around the framework and still enable the screen to close flat.

Screens can be made in a wide range of styles and shapes.

SOLID SCREENS

Inexpensive screens may be made by cutting solid shaped panels from a solid piece of board. However, this method is suitable only for a small screen: a large screen made from solid panels would be so unstable and heavy it would be almost impossible to move. The thickness of the screen side will be less than the traditional frame method as the board used will usually be no more than $\frac{3}{4}$ in (20 mm) thick.

Suitable boards are those which are stable enough to have the hinges mortised (housed) into the sides and to take staples or tacks easily. Plywood, medium density fiberboard (MDF) and particleboard (blockboard) all qualify.

FRAME SCREENS WITH FABRIC INSET

Screens may be made with fabric fitted inside a wooden frame, so that the frame is either partially covered with a fabric ruffle (frill) or not covered at all. The fabric will be fitted to the frame in one of three different ways.

1   The fabric may be gathered onto wires or brass rods fitted either inside the frame or onto the front and back of the frame.

2   The front and back fabrics may be made into a pad fitted "flat", anchored to the screen from the back with small pins. The pin marks will be covered with gimp or studs.

3   The fabric may be stretched onto a small wooden frame with a decorative wood frame around the outside.

Use a traditional jointed frame to make tall, elegant screens. For an
informal screen, fit fabric panels in three colorways into a smaller frame.

SCREEN WITH GATHERED FABRIC INSET

*E*asy to make in pretty floral or French provincial prints for cottage-style rooms, or in plain or shot silk for a more formal finish, these screens may be used to hide the television in a bedroom or livingroom, to hide pipes or towel racks in a bathroom or guest bedroom, or as corner "closets" to hide clothes hung on wall hooks in the corner of a small bedroom.

The wooden frame can be made from oak, pine, mahogany, or ash and waxed or sealed with a light, clear varnish or a light wood stain. For a more unusual and individual finish the frame may be lightly stained in a fantasy color or painted and finished with a freehand or stenciled design.

The bars holding the fabric may be fitted inside the frame opening or onto the fronts and backs of the frame. If plastic net wires are used, the fabric will need to be pulled over the ends to cover the screw and eye fittings. Small brass rods are a decorative alternative.

This method of making a gathered curtain fitted to a flexible or solid wire or rod can easily be adapted to fit open or glass cupboard door fronts.

Either find an old screen from an antique or junk shop or an auction house, or have one made to your dimensions. It is important that the joints are secure and invisible and that the edges have been sanded down enough to "round" the sharp corners slightly. Fit the bars, rods or wires and measure:
a) the diameter of the rod
b) the distance between the top of the top rod and
   the bottom of the bottom rod

c) the space above and below the rods which may be filled with a ruffle

d) the width of the rod

The width of fabric needed for each panel will be double the width of the rod (more for sheer fabrics). The length will be the vertical measurement of the gap to be filled plus three times the depth of the pocket for the rod and the ruffle (if any).

Materials

top fabric*

*If you are likely to need to wash the fabric panels regularly, choose a washable fabric, and pre-wash to be sure that no more shrinkage will occur.

---

1 Cut out fabric sections as planned. Mark the right and wrong sides if not obvious, and the top and bottom of each piece. Cut away the selvages.

2 Place one piece at a time, face down, on the worktable. Press over $1\frac{1}{2}$ in (4 cm) along the length of each side. Be careful not to pull the iron along the fabric or the edge will stretch. Press this fold under exactly in half to make a double hem of $\frac{3}{4}$ in (2 cm). Machine stitch along the fold. Repeat with each section.

3 Fold the turning allowance over double and press. Machine stitch in place very close to the edge of the hem, then stitch a parallel row far enough away from the first one to allow the rod to pass through easily. Press.

4 Thread the rods or wires through the openings and replace in the screen frame.

FIBERBOARD SCREEN

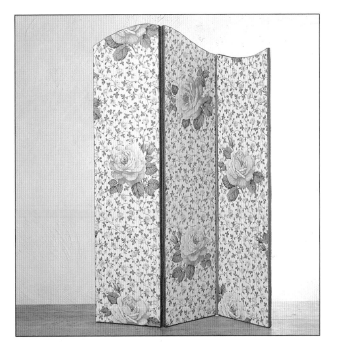

*T*his type of screen will probably be new so there will not be old fabric to remove. If there is, remove it and all hardware. Remove the hinges and keep hinges and screws together. Mark the hinge to screen position. To estimate the fabric for each panel, measure the height and width of the board and add $2\frac{1}{2}$ in (6 cm) for hems. A front and a back piece are needed for each panel.

Materials

top fabric for front and back of
  each panel
decorative gimp to go all around
  each panel
tack hammer and tacks or staple
  gun and staples
liquid fabric cement (glue)
lightweight interlining*
curved needle

*quantity as for top fabric

1 Cut out the interlining to fit the
front and back of the board panels.
Spread a thin layer of glue all around
the edges of the panel. Place the
interlining on the panel and press onto
the glue, keeping the fabric taut. Trim
away any excess fabric.

2 Cut out the top fabric panels. Place
the first section on the worktable

right side up. Place fabric on top, right
side up. Line up the grainline and the
pattern and pin to the interlining
around the outside edges. Temporary
tack at the corners and occasionally
along the sides to the outside edge of
the frame. Add more tacks until the
fabric is taut. The fabric should not
have any puckers, but should not be so
tight that the grain is distorted.

3 Hammer in the tacks. You may use
staples if you prefer.

4 Turn the screen section over and fit
the back fabric as above,
overlapping the fabrics on the sides and
cutting around the hinges.

5 Repeat with the other sections.

6 Fit the panels together again.
Hand-stitch gimp all around the
edges of each section, using a curved
needle, starting and finishing at the
bottom edge of the panel.

TRADITIONAL FRAME SCREEN

R emove any old fabrics and tacks. Remove hinges. Label the position of each hinge and keep hinges and screws together as there will never be two with exactly the same screw positions!

Measure the height and width of each panel adding $2\frac{1}{2}$ in (6 cm) to turn over and plan the fabric requirement. To add interest, use different fabrics front and back.

Materials

fabric for back and front of panels
inner covering – brown paper,
  white paper, interlining,
  blackout fabric or blackout
  paper, depending on the use for
  the screen and the background
  color of the fabric
liquid fabric cement (glue)
braid or rope to go all around
  each panel
tack hammer and tacks or staple
  gun and staples
gimp and gimp pins

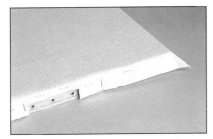

1 Cut out the inner covering and attach to the surface of the frame. This should be taut, without a single dent or pucker. Use glue, or tacks or staples to fit, depending on the materials used. Cut away around hinge positions.

2 Place the first frame panel on the worktable face up. Cut out the fabric panels and center the first one over the panel, lining up the grainline and any pattern with the outside and inside edges. Temporary tack at each corner, halfway along each side and then at approximately 12 in (30 cm) intervals. Tack the fabric to the outside edge of the frame, so that all tacks will be covered by the gimp. You may use staples if you prefer.

3 When you are satisfied that the fabric is as taut as possible without any stretch lines, hammer each tack in fully. Repeat with the other panels.

4 Turn the frame over and fit the back piece in the same way. Overlap the fabrics around the outside edges and cut away at the hinges. Repeat with the other panels.

5 Fit the frames together again. Spread glue around the outside edges of each section in turn and press the gimp in place to cover all raw edges and tacks or staples. Turn under the end of the gimp and secure with a gimp pin.

Variation ─────────────

A neat way to join the screen and hide the hinges back and front is to insert one strip of fabric before fitting together and another (or a piece of braid) after the hinges have been screwed in place. This is worthwhile for the expert finish it gives.

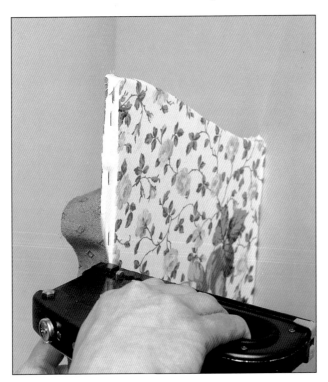

FIRESCREEN

There are many different styles and designs for firescreens and although this is certainly one of the most unusual I have found, the instructions for replacing the old fabric can be used and adapted as necessary for any firescreen or for any piece of furniture which has fabric enclosed within a wooden frame. This firescreen has three sliding panels to increase its width and height.

Materials

top fabric
brown paper to cover both sides
  of each panel
sharp craft knife
tack hammer and small tacks
small screwdriver and hammer to
  remove tacks
gimp or other trimming (optional)
panel pins
liquid fabric cement (glue)
  (optional)

1 Remove any old nails or screws which are projecting from the back. Consider the frame from the back and take note of the original method of assembly. It is important not to damage the woodwork by taking the wrong pieces apart first.

2 Carefully remove the nails or screws to release the sides and bottom of the frame. Place the frame pieces in order on one side, so that no mistakes can be made in reassembly.

3 Carefully remove the old fabric and any scraps which might have been left underneath. (Save anything that looks original or interesting for reference.) Use a sharp, fine craft knife to cut into the corners. Remove any tacks with a screwdriver and hammer, being careful not to damage the frame.

4 Measure each panel. Allow enough fabric to include any turn over and estimate the amount of fabric needed, taking the pattern position into account if relevant.

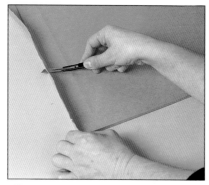

5 Cut paper to cover each panel front and back and glue in place around the outside edge.

6 Mark the center of each top, bottom, and side of the screen frame. Keeping the grainline straight, mark the center of each side of the fabric for the panel fronts. Tack the center points of the fabric to the center points marked on the screen. Temporary tack the corners in place.

7 Working on each side in turn, temporary tack in between the center tacks at 8, 4 and 2 in (20, 10 and 5 cm) intervals. Remove and replace tacks as necessary to give a good tight finish.

8 When you are satisfied that the fabric is taut but not over-stretched, hammer the tacks in fully. Trim away any excess fabric with a sharp knife.

9 Repeat to fit fabric to the back of the panels.

10 Fit the panels into the frame carefully and reassemble the woodwork in the same order as the frame was taken apart. Secure with panel pins as necessary.

11 Glue or tack the chosen gimp or trimming in place if needed.

INSET SCREEN

R emove the pins holding the inset frame in place. Cut away the cord or gimp and the old fabric. Remove pins or tacks. Treat the wood if necessary and repair any cracks. The panel will have a front and back, defined by the position of the hinges. Choose different fabrics for the two sides to add interest. Measure the height and width of each panel and estimate the amount of fabric needed, adding extra to turn over.

1 Cover the back and front of each frame section with brown paper. Glue or tape in place, so that the paper is taut and even with the outside edge of the frame all around.

2 Cut out the fabric front and back panels. Place the first frame on the worktable face up. Place a front fabric piece on the screen, lining up the pattern or grain to run vertically with the woodwork. Temporary tack at each corner and at 12 in (30 cm) intervals along the sides and top, keeping the tacks as close to the edge of the frame as possible. You do not want these to show when the frame is reassembled. You might prefer to use staples for this as it is easier to keep the staples very

close to the edge. Remove and replace tacks as necessary until the fabric is taut and the pattern lined up in all directions. The fabric must not be at all slack at this stage as it will soon sag if not fitted tightly.

3 Hammer in these tacks and tack in between until the fabric is firmly held onto the frame. Trim away the excess fabric.

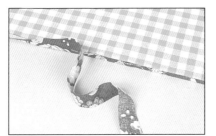

4 Fit the second fabric to the back in the same manner. Repeat with the other two frames.

5 Position the newly covered inner frames back into the outer frames. Use the small pins and hammer in approximately half their length to anchor the panels at each corner and

halfway along each side. Once the panels are held in place, add more pins, driving them in at an angle to secure the frames tightly to the front.

6 Spread a thin bead of glue around the outside edges of the back of the first panel. Press the cord close against the frame, covering all staple or tack marks. Start and finish at the bottom inner corner so that the join is in the least obvious place. Butt up cords and cut. Glue ends together. Repeat with the other panels.

Materials

fabric to cover the back and front
  of the panels
cord to go all around each of the
  panels front and back or back
  only
small pins to hold the frame back
  in place
tack hammer and tacks or staple
  gun and staples
brown paper
glue or tape

TENTED CEILINGS

*T*ented ceilings are both decorative and practical. Practically they can be used to great effect when a room is much too high for its width. This is a common problem in Georgian or early 20th century houses with high ceilings, which have been modified internally to make extra rooms.

A small bedroom or a long narrow hall can be made to seem much wider by lowering the ceiling. A fixed lowered ceiling is often uninteresting and unsuitable architecturally to the building, whereas a fabric ceiling will give warmth and character to a dull area.

Purely decorative tented ceilings can be made to emphasize a dining area in a large room, can completely cover a bedroom or luxury bathroom ceiling, or of course can be used on the underside of a bed canopy.

Plain silk will ruche or pleat beautifully – especially if a shot silk is used, the colors of which will change with the varied reflection of light.

Fabric can be pleated or gathered depending on the formality required and the type of fabric used. Any printed fabric must be cut and pleated carefully, so that the pattern makes concentric circles. This is not a project for the beginner! Stripes make very dramatic ceilings and are usually cut into shaped, flat panels and joined. If you really want to gather or pleat stripes, do a test area first as ruched stripes can look untidy and disappointing.

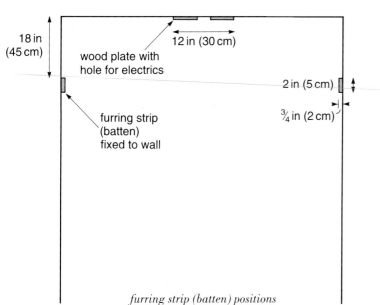

18 in (45 cm)

12 in (30 cm)

wood plate with hole for electrics

2 in (5 cm)

¾ in (2 cm)

furring strip (batten) fixed to wall

furring strip (batten) positions

All tented ceilings must be attached to a nailing strip which is at least 18 in (45 cm) below the ceiling. For a full tented ceiling, a furring strip (batten) can be fitted to the walls all around. If you are defining an area within an existing room, a false wall will have to be suspended from the ceiling to the bottom of the tenting. The inside of this new wall will be hidden by the fabric but the outside will need to be decorated to match the rest of the room. This new area does not need to be square or rectangular but can be hexagonal, octagonal, circular, or of mixed geometry.

Affix a circle of solid wood or board at least 12 in (30 cm) diameter to the ceiling at the exact center of the area to be tented for attaching the fabric. If there is an overhead light fixture, it will need to be rewired through a hole in the wood circle.

The instructions below are for the simplest type of tented ceiling covering a rectangular area. It can be adapted to suit any area, whether the ceiling of a room or of a bed. The photographs show a tented

ceiling contained within false walls.

Most tented ceilings will have a central light source, usually a chandelier. Make sure that the fixture is exactly centered, the wiring is complete, and the fittings are in place before the fabric is attached.

Canopied beds will usually come with fittings for the "ceiling". If the bed is antique and needs to have fittings made, seek the advice of a specialist.

To estimate the amount of fabric required, measure each side of the area to be covered, then measure the diagonal from center to corner. Multiply each side measurement by two-and-a-half to three to give the fabric fullness, and divide this figure by the width of your fabric to determine the number of widths of fabric required.

Example: Tenting an area 120 × 100 in (3 × 2.5 m) with fabric 52 in (1.3 m) wide:
Two sides 120 in (3 m) × 2.5 = 300 (7.5) ÷ 52 in (1.3 m) = 5.77 widths
Two sides 100 in (2.5 m) × 2.5 = 250 (6.25) ÷ 52 in (1.3 m) = 4.81 widths
So, 22 widths of fabric will be needed.

The length of each width will be of the longest dimensions (i.e. from the center diagonally to the corner). Add 4 in (10 cm) to this length for hems, etc., and multiply by the number of widths to get the total length of fabric needed.

Example: The diagonal is 80 in (2 m) plus 4 in (10 cm) allowance: 84 in (2.1 m) × 22 widths = 1848 in or 51⅓ yds (46.9 m) fabric required.

If the fabric is patterned, make an additional allowance for the repeat.

1 Cut the fabric into lengths as estimated and divide between the sides of the ceiling.

2 Working on one side at a time, divide the nailing strip into 20 equal segments. Using a pencil, mark these divisions on the inside of the strip

as a guide to placing the fabric.

3 Divide the total width of fabric for each side by 20 and mark with pins or pen. Find the center point on one of the fabric pieces and hold this against the center of the batten, so that it hangs down with the right side facing

out. Never have a seam at the center point. If there is an even number of widths, cut one of them in half and join to widths at each end. Hold the raw edge of the fabric so that it is approximately ¾ in (2 cm) above the bottom of the nailing strip, right side to the wall. Staple the center of the width of fabric to the marked center point using $\frac{1}{4}$ in (6 mm) staples.

4 Match up the adjacent division marks on fabric and nailing strip and staple in position.

This method of dividing both the nailing strip and the fabric into sections and matching the divisions is a simple way of making sure that you are using the same amount of fabric within each section and that the gathers will be evenly distributed.

5 Continue to work along the side, stapling the fabric in place on the nailing strip at each marked division. When a new width of fabric is added, fold in the selvage of the previous piece by approximately $1\frac{1}{2}$ in (4 cm) and lap the selvage of the next piece over the folded side of the previous piece, so that the selvages are not visible from the outside. The sides will not be joined, so the overlap must be adequate to prevent gaps between the widths.

6 Within each of the divisions, measure the center of each piece of fabric and staple to the halfway point on the batten and twice more within each section. (Judge the measurements by eye after the first few.)

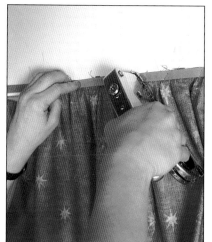

7 Place a length of back tack strip over the fabric, so that the bottom edge is $\frac{3}{8}$ in (1 cm) above either the bottom of the nailing strip or the wall. Gather the free fabric by hand and hold in place with the back tack. Staple at $\frac{1}{3}$ in (8 mm) intervals.

8 Mark the center circle in the ceiling into sections equal in number to the widths of fabric used. Again, starting with the center width of fabric on each side, gather each fabric width in your hand and staple, using $\frac{3}{8}$ in (10 mm) staples, to the allocated space on the wood. Make sure that the fabric joins are well overlapped.

Staple into the folds and then across to secure (approximately 10 staples per width of fabric). If you find that as you add more fabric the staples will not penetrate the thickness, use $1\frac{3}{8}$ in (35 mm) tacks to secure. Leave the excess fabric hanging down in the center of the ceiling.

When all the fabric is attached to the ceiling plate in the center, cut off the excess fabric to an even length.

9 Bunch up the fabric left hanging into a rosette making sure that the folds form an even circle around the light fixture. Hand stitch the rosette randomly but securely to the fabric gathers above.

Alternatively, cut spare fabric away and fit a large fabric button or rosette over the gap.

10 Make a ruche of fabric to cover the chandelier chain by cutting a piece of fabric twice the chain length and 12 in (30 cm) wide. Hold this around the chain and cable and pin together with both raw edges inside. Slipstitch along the length. Gather the top and lower edges to fit tightly around the chain. Twist the tube of fabric around the chain until the fullness looks right. Work the fabrics together at the top where the rosette and ruche meet. Keep working with the fabrics and pleating with your fingers until you are happy with the result. Stitch the top to the rosette.

11 Place a line of glue along the $\frac{3}{8}$ in (1 cm) of wood or wall which is still visible all around the bottom of the tented ceiling. Starting at one corner, position the cord on top of the glue to cover the gap. Press the cord into place with your hand, making sure that the glue holds it firmly. Keep the other hand under the cord to keep it level with the bottom of the nailing strip or against the wall. Glue the ends of the cord together to make a neat join. (This should be in the least conspicuous place.)

Materials

main fabric
staple gun
$\frac{1}{4}$ in (6 mm) and $\frac{3}{8}$ in (10 mm) staples
tack hammer and $1\frac{3}{8}$ in (35 mm) carpet tacks
back tack strip
sewing thread to match fabric
liquid fabric cement (glue)
cord to fit all around the bottom of the tenting, $\frac{1}{2}$ in (13 mm) diameter

DRESSING TABLES

Kidney-shaped dressing tables are now coming back into fashion after years of neglect. Most people seem to remember their childhood dressing table with nostalgia and memories of many hours spent writing letters and experimenting with make-up and home-made perfumes! Many are now re-covering the originals for their children.

The skirts can be fitted in a number of ways: they can be hooked to a track attached to the underside of the dressing table top enabling the curtains to pull to either side; attached to doors which open at either side to reveal rows of shelves; or attached to the front of the dressing table top with hook and loop tape, so that they will need to be lifted up rather than drawn for access.

If working with an old piece, strip away all the old fabric and remove all tacks. Remove any curtain track and reserve if in good condition. Repaint the insides and the drawer fronts. Line the drawers with paper. The following instructions are for a skirt fitted to a track or attached with hook and loop tape.

Materials

top fabric
lining, same amount as top fabric
interlining to cover the top
tack hammer and tacks or staple
  gun and staples
edgings or trims
hook and loop tape

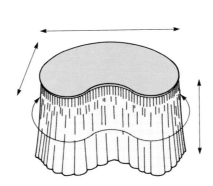

1 Measure at the widest points for the width and length of the top. Measure the skirt length and the distance around the dressing table which it is to cover. If the table will always be against a wall, no extra fullness needs to be allowed for the back, but if the back is in view it should be treated the same as the front. Allow at least double fullness: sheer fabric will need three to three-and-a-half times fullness. Add 5 in (13 cm) to the length for seam allowances. Plan the

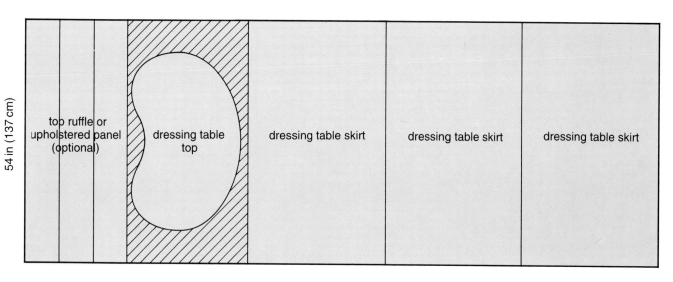

cutting layout – dressing table

pieces of fabric to fit within the width of your chosen fabric to calculate the amount of fabric needed, as shown in the diagram above.

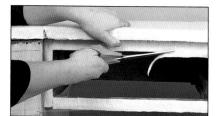

2   Cover the top with interlining. Press flat and staple or tack underneath, approximately $1\frac{1}{4}$ in (3 cm) in from the edge. Snip to enable the fabric to lie flat around the curves. Trim away excess fabric. Cover with the lining and fit in the same way.

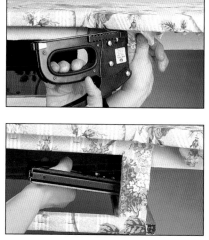

3   Position the top fabric, centering the pattern if necessary. Press. Pin

to secure around the edges. Fit underneath as before. Fit interlining and top fabric to any other surfaces, such as drawer fronts and surrounds.

4   Replace or renew the track or hook and loop tape.

5   To make up the skirt, cut the lengths of fabric and machine stitch the seams. Press flat, or make French seams if the fabric is sheer. Press the hem allowances to the wrong side along the sides and lower edge. Fold in half to make a double hem. Slipstitch with tiny stitches.

6   Make up the lining and press the seams flat. Press under a $1\frac{1}{4}$ in (3 cm) double hem at the lower edge and stitch by hand. Press the sides in by $1\frac{1}{4}$ in (3 cm). Fold in half to make a $\frac{5}{8}$ in (1.5 cm) double hem and slipstitch.

7   Place the top fabric on the worktable, right side down. Lay the lining over it, right side down if the top fabric is sheer, wrong side down if the top fabric is heavy enough that the lining seams will not be visible through it. Line up the seams and keep the lining hems level with the top fabric hems. Make sure that the lining does not drop below the top fabric. Measure up from the hemline to the finished skirt length. Mark this measurement at 12 in (30 cm) intervals with pins.

8   Fold over both fabrics to the wrong side along this line. Press. Stitch the heading tape in place. Pull up to the length needed to go all around the top. Fit to the track with hooks or to the top with hook and loop tape.

9   If the top is upholstered above the skirt, make a fabric edging to finish the raw edges, or attach an attractive gimp.

CUSHIONS

BOX CUSHIONS

The term box cushion simply means a cushion which has an edge strip, or boxing strip, between the top and bottom pieces. So, more accurately, they are "boxed" cushions. The main use for box cushions is to make the seat cushions for occasional chairs, armchairs, and sofas. Traditionally sofa backs were sprung and upholstered as a softer version of the seat. The seat would either be upholstered, usually with springs, though sometimes buttoned (e.g. Chesterfield style), or would have a single horsehair pad which would be covered with the top fabric to match or complement the sofa cover. Many sofas made now have boxed back and seat cushions. Box cushions can also be used as scatter pillows (cushions) on sofas, but as the addition of an edge strip makes a more bulky cushion, they need to be made small and decorative to place in front of a larger cushion or be placed on a side chair. Box cushions are also made for window seats, dining chair seats, and lawn chair seats or as a seat for a fabric-covered stool as shown on page 65.

The traditional hair seat pads are too firm for today's more comfortable lifestyle and so a variety of standard cushion fillings to suit varying needs have been adapted and are readily available. Duck or goosedown makes the most luxurious and longest-lasting cushion filling, but is also very expensive. The cost of 100% down fillings is high, so most people will opt for a mixture of down and chicken feather. The most common is 40% down 60% feather, which gives a mediocre filling which will need plumping up regularly. Try to find at least a 60% down 40% feather filling for a cushion which will plump up satisfactorily.

Whereas down will stay fluffy for years, feathers uncurl and go flat. Once this has happened the cushion filling should be replaced. Always overstuff the cushions initially to allow for the inevitable flattening which will occur once the cushions are in regular use.

Some people dislike the crumpled look which a soft filling gives, in which case a firm filling can be used. The most common will be a piece of foam with a thick Dacron wrap to soften the seat. Foam cushions are priced according to the quality and construction of the cushion. The best and most comfortable foam cushions have been carefully constructed from several layers of foam in varying weights with a hard center core and gradually softer layers. These cushions still have the firm look but are very comfortable to sit on. The least expensive single foam cushions are either so hard that you sit rather stiffly on top of them or so soft that they quickly flatten and lose shape.

A recent solution to this problem is the creation of a cushion with a good quality foam interior with a quilted feather wrap. This cushion strikes a balance between the look of the seat cushion, its comfort, and its maintenance, but it is only available from certain furniture manufacturers. Another solution which is much less expensive and more widely available is a filling made with a mixture of fiber and feathers, or fiber only. Neither of these are long-term solutions as the fiber will mat down and the edges which have been sat on regularly will become misshapen. Many people compromise by having some sort of foam cushion on the seat and feather cushions on the back, which are more comfortable to sink into. Cushion fillings should either be bought with long-term use in mind or be changed and serviced regularly.

T o M a k e a B o x C u s h i o n C o v e r

Materials

top fabric
piping to go all around the top
  and bottom of the cushion*
zipper, the length of the back
  edge of the cushion plus 12 in
  (30 cm)
pad

*see step 1 below

1 To estimate the amount of fabric needed, measure the longest and the widest points of the pad. Add $1\frac{1}{2}$ in (4 cm) seam allowance. Two pieces are needed with these measurements. Measure for the edge strip starting at one side approximately 4 in (10 cm) from the back of the pad, across the front and along the other side to 4 in (10 cm) from the back. Add $\frac{3}{4}$ in (2 cm) either side of the width for seam allowance, and $1\frac{1}{2}$ in (4 cm) to the length. The rest of the edge strip will need to be cut in two pieces for the zipper. Cut the two strips the length of the remaining edge strip plus $1\frac{1}{2}$ in (4 cm) seam allowances and half the width of the edge strip plus $1\frac{1}{2}$ in (4 cm) seam and opening allowance. Make paper patterns of these pieces (top, bottom, edge strip).

2 Place these pieces on the fabric to see how they fit into the width. Any motifs should be centered and the pattern should read from front to back. The edge strip should be cut so that the pattern follows through and matches on either side of the piping. If possible, make the top and bottom cushion panels so that they are reversible.

3 When cutting piping strips, try to have as few joins as possible, but also try to cut them from the fabric between the other pieces when possible. Make up the piping (see page 18).

4 Cut out the top and bottom pieces as planned, then place flat on the worktable, right sides exactly together.

Cut notches on all four sides for matching. Use single, double and triple V cuts at 4–8 in (10–20 cm) intervals.

5 Starting on the back edge, pin piping to the right side of the fabric, all around both the top and the bottom pieces. Pin so that the stitching line on the piping casing is on the seam allowance. Pin the corners (see page 18). Join the piping at the back (see page 19). Machine stitch in place along the piping stitching line.

6 To make up the zipper insert, fold under the two long sides of the edge strip sections $\frac{3}{4}$ in (2 cm). (If patterned, make sure you fold the matching sides.) Place the zipper so that the slide is $\frac{3}{4}$ in (2 cm) in from one end and the opposite end extends further than the corresponding edge strip end. Machine stitch in place.

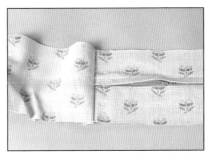

7 Machine stitch one short end of the edge strip to the slide end of the zipper edge strip with the zipper closed. Open the zipper slightly.

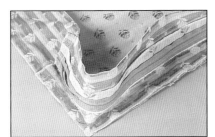

8 Pin the zipper edge strip/main edge strip seam to the cushion front on one of the sides, 4 in (10 cm) from the back, right sides together. Continue to pin the edge strip to the cushion front around all four sides. Match the seamlines of the cover and edge strip and pin to the piping

seamline. Clip into the corners, right up to the seamlines to make a good square corner. Keep the cover flat on the worktable and make sure that the two layers are pinned evenly. Where the zipper strip and the main edge strip meet, pin together and stitch the short seam before finishing the pinning. Trim seam allowances.

9 Machine stitch all around close to the piping as before. Check from the front that the first piping stitching line is not visible. If it is, stitch around again from the other side, making sure this stitching line is inside the first.

10 Pin the cushion back to the other side of the edge strip. Start at the back and, matching the seamlines, pin along the piping stitching line. Match up the notches by scoring a pinline from a notch on the stitched side across the edge strip following the fabric grain. This point should match the corresponding notch on the other piece of the cover. At each corner score a pinline from the stitched corner to the opposite side of the edge strip. Clip into the seam allowance. Machine stitch all around, double stitching around the cuts on each corner, and reinforcing the corner by stitching at an angle across the corner.

11 Trim the seam allowance to $\frac{5}{8}$ in (1.5 cm). Cut across the corners to within $\frac{1}{4}$ in (6 mm) of the stitching. Trim the seam allowances. Open up the zipper. Turn the cover to the right side. Shape each corner with a point turner or the point of your scissors. Press all over. Lightly press the seam allowances away from the edge inset. Place the pad inside the cover, checking that the filling fits right into each corner.

*F*ITTED *K*NIFE-*E*DGE (*S*QUAB) *C*USHIONS

*F*itted knife-edge (squab) cushions are covered, thin (almost flat) cushion pads, which fit wooden or cane chair seats to make them more comfortable. They are made to fit the chair seat exactly, usually from two pieces of fabric, stitched together with piping around the edge. They are often buttoned. The pad can vary from less than 1 in (2.5 cm) to 2 in (5 cm) in depth and would traditionally have been made from hair or straw. Today we use either foam wrapped in polyester batting (wadding) or a purchased hair pad, either horsehair or the more easily available and much

less costly rubberized hair. Thinner knife-edge cushions (simple squabs) are for ordinary bedroom and kitchen chair seats. Box cushions (boxed squabs) will be from $1\frac{1}{3}$ in (3.5 cm) to 2 in (5 cm) in depth (see page 114).

Choose the depth by looking at the proportions of the chair to make sure that the balance will not be destroyed by having a pad which is either too thin or too thick and by sitting on the chair to find the most comfortable seat height. The following method uses a foam pad, see "Fitted Box Cushions" for details on hair pads.

Materials

foam pad cut to seat template
(see step 1), maximum depth
1½ in (4 cm)
lightweight batting (wadding) to
wrap around pad
curtain lining to cover both sides
top fabric
contrast fabric for ties and piping
if desired
piping cord
zipper (see step 6)
10 buttons (optional)
newspaper or other scrap paper
masking tape
pencil with soft lead or felt-tip pen
heavy-duty needle
buttonhole or upholstery thread

1 Cut a piece of paper larger than the chair seat. Tape to secure on the two sides. Fold the paper back on itself around the back and legs, following the seat line. Tape down. Cut neatly around the leg to the sides of the seat. With the side of the pencil lead against the outside edge of the chair seat, run the pencil around the other three sides. Remove paper and cut the seat template to shape.

2 Cut out one piece of batting (wadding) to fit the seat pad exactly and place on top of the pad. Place the pad onto the remaining piece of batting (wadding), and fold up over the sides to meet the top piece. Feather out, so that it clings to itself around the edges.

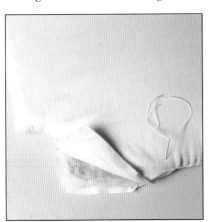

3 Cut out two pieces of lining using the template and adding half the

side depth plus ⅜ in (1 cm) seam allowance all around. With right sides together, machine stitch around the leg cut-outs and three sides, allowing ⅝ in (1.5 cm) for the seam. (This will pull the pad in enough to round the edges.) Turn the lining cover right side out. Slip the pad into the cover and slipstitch closed.

4 Cut out two pieces of fabric for the top and bottom of the cushion, allowing 1 in (2.5 cm) all around the template. Place the two pieces flat on the worktable, right sides together. Cut three or four notches into the seam allowances to use for re-matching later.

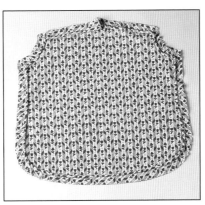

5 Make up enough piping to go around the outer edge of the cushion. Pin the piping all around one of the pieces, clipping into curves and into the leg cut-outs, so that the piping lies flat (see page 18).

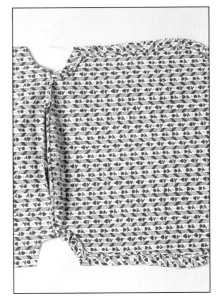

6 Match the top and bottom again, right sides together. Machine stitch

together for ¾ in (2 cm) at each side of the back edge, leaving a gap for the zipper. Fit the zipper into the gap by hand or machine.

7 Make up four ties (see page 17). Pin two ties to fit either side of the chair leg and machine stitch to secure.

8 Undo the zipper slightly. Pin the top piece to the bottom piece all around, right sides together, pinning to the piping stitching line.

9 Machine stitch together. Turn right side out. Press. Insert the pad, making sure that the corners are well filled. With your hand inside the cover, finger press the seam allowances downward. The cover will fit much more smoothly if the seams are lying straight.

10 To mark the button positions if fitting, find the center of the pad and mark four more points in a square around this center, checking that the vertical, horizontal, and diagonal lines are equal to each other. Turn over and repeat on the underside.

11 Using the heavy-duty needle and buttonhole or upholstery thread, push through the pad from the bottom to the top. Thread through one button and push the needle back through the pad to within ⅛ in (3 mm) of the first hole. Thread on another button underneath, tie the threads together and pull tightly. Knot two to three times to secure. Repeat at the remaining four button positions.

FITTED BOX (BOXED SQUAB) CUSHIONS

*M*ake the template for the seat cushion (see page 117, step 1). Make patterns for the edge strip and zipper inset (see page 115, step 1). Decide which sort of ties to use and whether you will have any other decorative finish. Plan whether the piping will be in self or contrast fabric. Plan the fabric for the five pieces, top, bottom, edge strip and upper and lower zipper insets on the worktable or on graph paper to establish the amount needed. The pad is made with rubberized hair covered with batting (wadding) to soften it. A layer of interlining holds the shape and adds more padding. The final covering of lining holds it firmly together.

Materials

rubberized hair, 2 in (5 cm) deep, cut to template

2 pieces of cotton batting (wadding), cut $\frac{1}{4}$ in (6 mm) larger than the template

2 pieces of curtain interlining, one cut to template, one cut $1\frac{1}{2}$ in (4 cm) larger

top fabric

curtain lining or plain cotton (see step 3)

contrast fabric if needed

piping or flanged cord

zipper

10–14 buttons

heavy-duty needle

buttonhole or upholstery thread

1 Place one layer of cotton batting (wadding) on the worktable. Place the hair pad on it and the other layer of batting (wadding) on top. Press the pieces together. The fibers in the pad will cling to the batting (wadding).

2 Place the smaller piece of interlining over the batting (wadding) and press down. Place the larger piece of interlining underneath. Fold the border of interlining up onto the sides of the pad. Trim excess interlining at corners. Hand sew all raw edges together, pulling the pad in slightly to reduce the depth to $1\frac{1}{2}$ in (4 cm) and make a firm pad.

3 Cut three pieces of lining: two pieces for the top and bottom $\frac{3}{8}$ in (1 cm) larger than the template all around, and one strip to fit all around the sides $2\frac{1}{2}$ in (6 cm) wide. Pin the edge strip to the top and bottom pieces,

matching corners carefully and taking up the $\frac{3}{8}$ in (1 cm) seam allowance. Leave the back open on one side of the edge strip. Machine stitch along pin lines. Turn right side out and slip over the pad. Slipstitch the back opening together.

4 Cut out the fabric as planned with $\frac{3}{4}$ in (2 cm) seam allowance all around. Place the top and bottom pieces, right sides together. Cut notches, approximately two per side, to help re-matching later. Make up enough piping to go around the cushion twice (or use flanged cord). Pin and machine stitch the piping all around the bottom piece on the right side of the fabric (see page 18). Repeat to pipe the top piece.

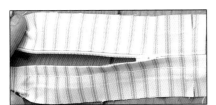

5 To make up the zipper inset, cut two pieces of top fabric the length of the back of the pad and $2\frac{1}{2}$ in (6 cm) wide. Press under the seam allowances of $\frac{3}{4}$ in (2 cm) on both sides. Machine stitch the zipper between the two.

6 Make the ties from four pieces of fabric 3 in (7.5 cm) wide and 16 in (40 cm) long (see page 17).

7 Pin both ties to each end of the zipper inset, if there is no leg cut-out, if there is a leg cut-out, pin one tie to each side of it, then machine stitch one end of this inset to one short end of the long edge strip, right sides together. Pin this seam to the bottom piece to line up with the back corner. (The zipper flap should face downward on the finished cushion.) Pin the edge strip to the bottom piece all around, matching

the seamlines. Snip into the seam allowance at the corners. At the back, seam the end of the zipper inset to the end of the edge strip.

8 Machine stitch along the pinned line, as close to the piping cord as possible. Turn the cover around to the front and, if you can see any of the piping stitching line, re-stitch from the cover side, inside the previous stitching line.

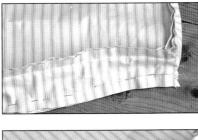

9 Pin the other side of the edge strip onto the top cover piece, matching seamlines and notches. Use a pin to score a line along the depth of the edge strip from one notch to its opposite to check that they are accurately aligned. At each corner fold the edge strip to line up with the cover corner already stitched and clip the seam allowance at the center of this fold to form a sharp corner on the top cover. Machine stitch all around.

10 Trim the seam allowances on the inside. Check that the ties are well secured.

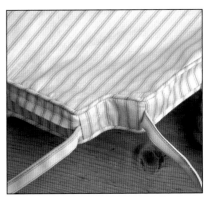

11 Turn the cover right side out. Finger press the seam allowances in the same direction and use a pin to pull the corners square. Press. Insert the pad.

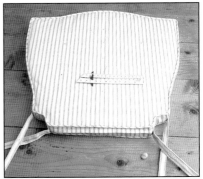

12 Plan the positioning for the buttons on the template first. Measure the distances between the button positions and transfer to the cushion top. Mark with pencil or crossed pins. Mark exactly the same positions on the bottom piece.

Using the heavy-duty needle and strong thread, sew on the buttons (see page 117, step 11).

Note: To clean these pads, cut threads, remove the cover and clean according to manufacturer's instructions. Replace pad when clean and re-position the buttons using the same holes.

Variations of ties and finishes ___
The following pages show a selection of different decorative treatments for these cushions.
A–B: Plain fitted cover with harmonizing plain chintz piping and long, narrow ties.
C: Harmonizing piping and large self bows.
D: Strong contrast piping, buttoning and simple

ties with contrast buttons.
E: Self piping and self ties with contrast button.
F: Contrast tiny piping and buttoning, self ties, piped to match cover.
G–I: Contrast piping and buttons, bows lined in contrast color, tied three ways.
J: Close-up of button detail in ties.

A

B

C

D

E

F

G

H

I

J

WINDOW SEAT CUSHIONS

Although under the heading of "boxed cushions", this type of cushion does not have a continuous inset edge strip, but it can be termed as such because the pad is boxed. This type of window seat cushion needs to have a hard filling to look right, so feathers and down are not suitable. Originally the pad would have been made of layers of horsehair stitched together through the middle, and into a roll all around the edge. Old pads can easily be made good with some slight restructuring and some additional hair. Poorer households would have had straw pads. The construction was similar to that of a flat mattress. Suitable alternatives today are foam with a Dacron cover or rubberized hair with a cover of cotton batting (wadding). Make a paper template of the cushion area.

TO MAKE A SIMPLE PAD

Materials

1 piece of rubberized hair 1–2 in (2.5–5 cm) deep, cut to template
curtain interlining to cover
cotton batting (wadding), cut to the length of the template and twice the width, plus 1 in (2.5 cm) all around to turn under
curtain lining or plain cotton to cover

1 Wrap the hair pad with the cotton batting (wadding), so that the raw edges are at the back and sides, leaving the front edges smooth and seam free. Smooth out and trim away excess, so that the pad is now totally enclosed.

2 Cover the batting (wadding) with the interlining. Pull the top and bottom together at the back, so that the edges butt together and the pad is quite firm. Whip (oversew) the raw edges together along the back. Cut an edge strip to fit each end of the pad and stitch around, keeping the pad tight.

3 Cover this pad with lining in the same way, with an edge inset at either end. Turn in the raw edges and slipstitch across the long side and all around the two short sides to enclose the pad.

To Make the Cushion
Cover

Materials

cushion pad
top fabric
zipper the length of the back of
    the cushion pad
buttons or tufts
heavy-duty needle
buttonhole or upholstery thread

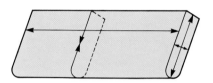

1 Measure all around the width of
    the pad and add $1\frac{1}{2}$ in (4 cm) seam
allowance. Measure the longest side of
the pad and add the seam allowance as
before. Measure the length and width of
the side inset and add the same seam
allowance (see diagram). Plan the fabric
layout (one main piece and two inset
pieces) on the worktable or on graph
paper to work out the amount needed. If
the fabric is patterned, decide how it
should be best positioned on the cover.

2 Cut the fabric pieces as planned. If
    the cushion pad is shaped, make a
template and place it on the fabric
piece. Add seam allowances and cut
out. Cut the inset strip so that one end is
rounded, the other straight. The straight
end will be the back of the inset.

3 Press $\frac{3}{4}$ in (2 cm) under on both
    long sides of the main piece.
Machine stitch the first side of the
zipper along the length which will be
the bottom of the cushion. The slide
should be just inside the $\frac{3}{4}$ in (2 cm)
seam allowance and the other end
should extend into the seam allowance.
Pin the opposite side over the zipper,
covering the teeth evenly. Open up the
zipper and machine stitch in place.

4 Turn the cover to the inside. Close
    the zipper a short way. Pin the
zipper to the center back of the edge
inset, right sides together. Match
seamlines and cut into seam allowance
at back corners, so that they lie flat. Pin
along each side toward the rounded
end. Clip into seam allowance where
necessary to ease the cover around the

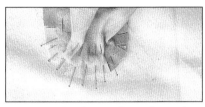

inset. Pin closely at right angles to the
seam to give a good, pleat-free fit.

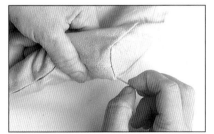

5 Repeat with the other side.
    Machine stitch around both sides.
Trim the seam allowance back to $\frac{5}{8}$ in
(1.5 cm). Neaten the seam. Turn right
side out. Use a pin to pull the seam out
to make a neat, rounded line.

6 Press the seams so that the seam
    allowances all face in the same
direction. Press the cover. Insert the
pad, making sure that the corners and
front fit tightly.

7 To mark the positions for buttons,
    use the paper template to plan a
suitable pattern. Place the buttons on
the cushion to check the placement.
When you are happy with the button
positions, mark the top and bottom with
pencil, washable ink, or crossed pins.

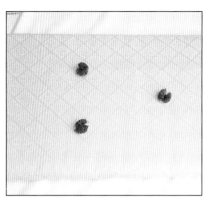

8 Using strong thread and a large
    needle, push through the cover and
pad from one marked position on the
bottom of the pad to the corresponding
one on the top. Thread on the button or
tuft. Push the needle back through and
into the button or tuft on the back. Knot
the threads together and pull tight.
Secure with a triple knot.

9 To remove the cover for cleaning,
    cut the threads holding the
buttons, unzip the cover and clean.
Replace the buttons using the same
holes as before.

LLOYD LOOM CHAIRS

*L*loyd Loom chairs are a type of woven wicker chair made in England in the early part of the century and currently enjoying a huge revival. The old, painted, and faded colors and comfortable shapes are now much sought after for use in the garden, indoor and outdoor sunrooms, bathroom, and as bedroom chairs. They have the advantages of being comfortable for short-term seating and taking up little space. The overall shape is neat and the chairs can be unobtrusive.

Damaged wicker can be repaired by a specialist (in England the chair can be sent to one of the Lloyd Loom revival manufacturers). The wicker can be repainted if desired but the worn, faded colors of the old chairs add to their charm.

The techniques described below can be applied to other types of rattan furniture.

Remove the seat from the chair, turn it over and check its construction. There are two possible types of seat. The first will have a wood base with a piece of foam stuck on top, usually about 4 in

(10 cm) in depth, and the whole covered in fabric. The wood base rests on a "shelf" all around the inside of the chair. The second type of seat is fully sprung. You will be able to feel the springs beneath a soft hair pad which makes the top of the seat, and the base will be covered in burlap (hessian). You may need to remove several layers of fabric before you find the original cushion. This cushion will also rest on a shelf but the ledge will be wider than for the cushions with wood bases. The following instructions cover both types of seat.

As these cushion covers are fixed in place, slipcovers (loose covers) may be made to cover them, or the base may be made shallower and a box cushion with a removable, washable cover placed on top to take the wear.

Measure the overall width and length of the fabric required. Decide whether you will keep the seat high or whether you will make a shallower seat pad and have a washable box cushion on top, and plan your fabric requirements accordingly.

To Re-Cover a Wood Seat

Materials

fabric as estimated
muslin (calico) to cover
polyester batting (wadding)
tack hammer and tacks or staple
 gun and staples
foam or rubberized hair pad, cut
 ⅝ in (1.5 cm) larger all around
 than the wood base
white (fabric-to-wood) glue
black cambric (platform cloth)

1 Remove the old foam and discard, as this will be deteriorating and crumbly. Spread a thin layer of glue on the top of the wood base and center the new foam on it. Leave to dry.

2 Cover the top and sides with two layers of batting (wadding).

3 Cover with muslin (calico) to fit just under the base. Staple or tack to the underside, pulling tightly, so that the foam is now the same size as the wood. Start at the center front, and work out to either side, tacking at 2 in (5 cm) intervals. Pull to the back and secure the center back and toward the corners. Secure the centers of each side and toward the corners. The front corners will need to be folded to make an inverted dart and the back corners pulled into small gathers on the underside. Pull the fabric tightly enough to eliminate puckers on the cushion top and sides. Trim away the excess fabric neatly underneath.

4 Position the top cover, centering any pattern, and tack in place as for the muslin (calico). Tap the tacks in only halfway to start with, so that they may be easily adjusted as the fabric stretches and forms the shape of the cushion.

5 Cut a piece of cambric (platform cloth) slightly larger than the pad, fold under the edges and tack in place all around, ⅜ in (1 cm) from the edge to enclose all raw edges.

6 If you have decided to have a separate box cushion, make up following the directions on page 115, making sure that the pattern at the center of the cushion lines up with that on the pad.

To Re-Cover a Sprung Seat

Materials

burlap (hessian)
upholstery pins
linterfelt or cotton batting
 (wadding)
muslin (calico)
top fabric

1 Remove the old burlap (hessian) and shake out all dust. Remove the top pad carefully and put to one side. The springs will be individual coils, but wired together in a framework following the shape of the chair seat.

2 Cover the top of the springs with a new piece of burlap (hessian) and stitch the springs to it (see page 14).

3 Pull the burlap (hessian) to the underside of the spring unit and pin all around with upholstery pins, so that the springs are totally enclosed in burlap (hessian) and are firm but not under pressure. Stitch in place. Stitch the bottom of each spring to the burlap (hessian) as above.

4 Place the hair pad back on top. If this is very flat, tease out the hair. Stitch the edge of the pad to the burlap (hessian) all around.

5 Cover the top and sides with a thin layer of linterfelt, cover this with muslin (calico) and stitch it to the bottom edge all around.

6 Position the top cover, centering any pattern. Pin along the bottom edge to hold in place. Work all around the cushion, adjusting as necessary to achieve a smooth edge.

7 Pleat the back corners in two or three places to fit around the curve. Make inverted pleats at the front corners and handstitch to close.

8 Trim the fabric so that ⅜ in (1 cm) can be turned under all around and stitched to the burlap (hessian) just inside the bottom edge. Fold under and stitch in place.

DECK CHAIRS

*D*eck chair covers are usually made from very tough canvas which is specially made so that it will not shrink if left out in the rain, or stretch when sat on, or fade in direct sunlight. This canvas can be bought in "deck chair" width from some fabric stores.

These deck chairs have been covered in a readily available strong ticking as a first cover, with a brightly colored and boldly designed print, as a removable lightly padded top cover.

The top cover is not intended to withstand rainfall and bright sunlight so should be removed when not in use.

Materials

under fabric as estimate
top fabric and lining for the pad
$\frac{1}{2}$ in (13 mm) tacks and tack
    hammer
grosgrain ribbon or seam binding
    (twice the length of the top pad
    and twice the width, plus $1\frac{3}{4}$ yds
    (1.6 m)

1 Remove the old cover, and measure to estimate the amount of new under fabric required. No seam allowances will be needed if you are using "deck chair" fabric. If you are using wider fabric which will need to be cut down, allow for side hems of $1\frac{1}{2}$ in (4 cm) on each side.

For the seat pad measure from the top bar to the seat bar allowing for the seat curve and the width of the old cover. Allow $\frac{5}{8}$ in (1.5 cm) seam allowance all around. Plan to cut two or three covers from the fabric width.

2 If you are using "deck chair" fabric, cut to the length of the old cover and tack into place as before.

Otherwise, turn in the $1\frac{1}{2}$ in (4 cm) side hems and press. Fold under to give a $\frac{3}{4}$ in (2 cm) double hem and machine stitch to secure. Tack onto the chair frame. Tack near, but not into, the old tack holes, along the same line.

3 Place the lining fabric on the worktable right side down. Press. Place the interlining on top, and press. Place the top fabric over, right side up, to sandwich the interlining and press. Pin all around to hold the three pieces together securely.

4 To quilt, decide the size of the square you would like and mark the quilting lines with a long ruler and pins. Baste (tack) the three pieces together along the pin lines with contrasting thread. Machine stitch along the basted (tacked) lines. Remove basting (tacking) threads and press.

5 Cut two pieces of binding the length of the cover plus 32 in (80 cm) and two pieces the width of the cover plus 32 in (80 cm). Fold the binding in half and place the foldline at the edge of the fabrics so that both sides of the binding are equal. Pin along the

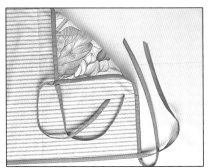

width of the pad at top and bottom, leaving 16 in (40 cm) at each side. Machine stitch close to the binding edge. Machine stitch the tapes together beyond the pad and enclose the raw edges. Repeat with the sides. Press.

6 Tie the cover to the deck chair frame at each corner.

DIRECTOR'S CHAIRS

Director's chairs, whether new or antique, are straightforward to re-cover. The fitting method may be different from the one shown, but the basic method of securing fabric to wood bars will remain the same. Sometimes the fabric cover will be tacked in place to wood or riveted to metal rods or bars. Most commonly the cover is removable and slotted into a groove cut into the wood bars, secured with a bolt and fly nut.

Remove the old seat and back covers. Make sure that you note how to re-fit them.

Measure each piece and add seam allowances where necessary to estimate the amount of fabric needed. If the fabric chosen is very soft, make sure that the lining is tightly woven to prevent premature stretching of the top cover. Use heavy-duty canvas or sailcloth if you do not want to make up this double layer.

Materials

top fabric as estimated
lining for the seat and back
interlining for padding
basting (tacking) thread in
 contrasting color

1 Pin the old back piece onto the top fabric, centering any pattern. Add seam allowances all around and cut out. (If the old cover has stretched considerably, make allowance for this by cutting the piece smaller. Cut the

interlining to the same size.

2 Cut the lining, adding the same seam allowances top and bottom but none at the sides.

3 Place the interlining on the worktable. Place the top fabric exactly over it, right side up, and the lining, right side down, on top of these two pieces. Pin together all around. Machine stitch along the top and bottom on the seamline.

4 Trim the interlining very close to the stitching line, and so that it lines up with the lining at each side. Trim the lining seam allowance to half. Press the seams flat. Turn right side out and press along the seamline.

5 Mark the pad into squares or diamonds for quilting and baste

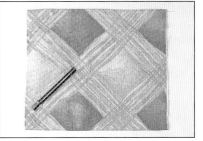

(tack), see page 126.

6 Machine stitch along the basted (tacked) lines. Always stitch in the same direction to avoid distorting the fabric. Knot all threads, remove basting (tacking) threads, and press.

7 From the back, fold the side hems over to enclose the metal or plastic rod. Turn under the raw edges. Machine stitch as close to the rod as possible. If this hem is too bulky it will not fit back into the groove.

SLIPCOVERS
(LOOSE COVERS)

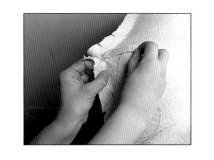

SLIPCOVER (LOOSE COVER) MAKING

*I*n the past slipcovers (loose covers) were considered to be inferior to upholstery. The upholsterer's skill was always well appreciated and indeed the only way to become an upholsterer was by serving a long apprenticeship in one of the few traditional upholstery workshops. The upholsterer not only would make the stuffing and springing for the furniture from the joiner's frame up, re-cover, and restore damaged and worn items of furniture, but would also attend to any draperies for the household. Upholsterers would employ seamstresses to stitch the work that they had cut. The seamstress was very much an assistant and would not be allowed to cut the cloth.

The upholsterer who did specialize in cutting slipcovers (loose covers) appreciated the advantages of being able to leave the workshop periodically to visit his clients' homes in order to cut the covers. The cut pieces would be very carefully marked and given to a seamstress to stitch together. An upholsterer and his seamstress would usually work together for many years.

In larger households slipcovers were made by the household staff to protect the expensive fabrics which were upholstered onto dining chairs, occasional chairs, and sofas. The covers for dining chairs would often have the family initials or insignia embroidered onto the front and would remain in place for all but the most important occasions.

Slipcovers in plain cottons were also made to cover over all upholstered furniture, sometimes including the wood and curtain drapes as well, as a protection against dust when the family went away or up to town for "the Season".

As fewer household staff became available the practicalities of having removable covers ensured that slipcovers were gradually considered in their own right as an acceptable alternative to fully upholstered furniture. More expensive fabrics and elaborate finishes were used. Sofas and chairs would still be upholstered in best fabric, usually in dark colors, but a set of removable covers would also be made in printed cotton chintz designed for summer use.

At the turn of the century, covers in printed or striped cottons would be put on after the "great Spring Cleaning" and removed in the fall, to reveal the heavier, darker upholstery for winter use. At the same time lightweight summer curtains would be replaced by the heavy winter ones. I suppose this was particularly useful when homes were heated solely with coal fires, but I feel it would be a good practice to re-introduce to allow seasonal changes in our own homes.

Slipcovers (loose covers) generally suit rooms which are comfortable rather than sophisticated. They can be made to fit sofas and chairs so closely as to be almost indistinguishable from the upholstery, or they can be made in varying degrees of "looseness" to suit the fabrics and general style of the room.

Old, lumpy but comfortable sofas are not improved by firm re-upholstery and can easily become uncomfortable if the seats and backs are upholstered too tightly. Slipcovers (loose covers) in printed or self-patterned linens, or woven cottons, will suit this type of sofa or chair much better.

Fabrics most suitable for slipcovers (loose covers) should be washable and not so springy that the folds and pin marks fall out quickly. Printed or plain cottons, linen, cotton/linen/nylon blend, cotton-acrylic mix, and woven damasks are all suitable fabrics. Linen and linen-cotton fabrics have a built-in flexibility and will resist tearing. Linen can feel slightly damp to touch and does not take dye into its core, so that printed linen will wear to reveal the center off-white core of the thread.

Close-woven cotton fabrics are harder wearing than the popular linen/cotton blends but have the disadvantage that they will show creases across the cushions. Cotton will tear easily if caught by a buckle or a heel, whereas linen will give a little – often just enough to prevent permanent damage.

Check the "rub test" of your chosen fabric to assess the long-term wearability. Average "rub tests" are between 15,000 and 60,000.

Choose the quality and finish of your fabric to suit the piece of furniture and its situation. Obviously a much harder-wearing fabric will be needed for a family room sofa than for a delicate guest bedroom side chair.

If you are unsure whether a fabric has been fully shrunk, over-cut each piece by $1\frac{1}{2}$–2 in (4–5 cm) and wash at 88° F/30° C in plain water. Dry flat and press while still slightly damp.

C L E A N I N G

To wash your cover, follow the manufacturer's instructions for the fabric and half dry as recommended. Press carefully. Press into the seams from either side with the point of the iron. Do not press over the seams as they will usually have at least four layers of fabric and it would mark the top cover with a ridge. Slip back onto the chair while still damp. Finger press all the seam allowances in the same direction (usually to the back and downward, although sometimes the shape of the chair demands otherwise). Pull the cover into shape over the curves and corners while still damp. Press the cover while on the chair if necessary. To press the dust ruffle (valance) after the cover has been fitted, plug your iron into an outlet (socket) positioned close to the chair, make a plain cotton pad and place it on a low stool, then lift up the ruffle (valance) piece by piece and press.

E S T I M A T I N G   T H E   F A B R I C

Look at the chair or sofa which you wish to cover and try to visualize it finished. Decide whether you prefer a plain or patterned fabric; whether a print or weave; whether the pattern should be large or small; where the piping lines should be; whether you want to emphasize a particular line or "lose" another; whether the piping should be harmonizing,

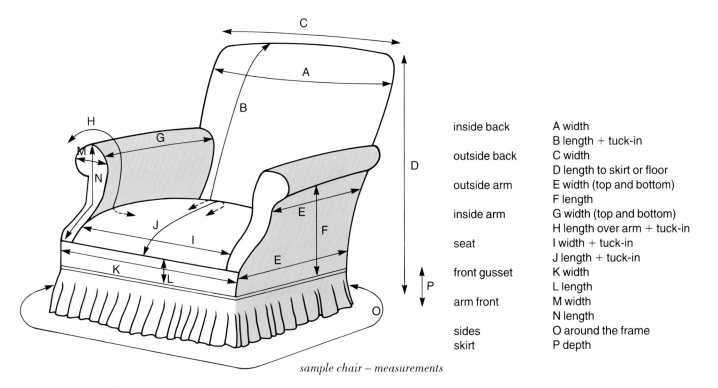

inside back	A width
	B length + tuck-in
outside back	C width
	D length to skirt or floor
outside arm	E width (top and bottom)
	F length
inside arm	G width (top and bottom)
	H length over arm + tuck-in
seat	I width + tuck-in
	J length + tuck-in
front gusset	K width
	L length
arm front	M width
	N length
sides	O around the frame
skirt	P depth

sample chair – measurements

contrasting, or of the main fabric; how formal the chair will be; whether the dust ruffle (valance) should be ruffled, box pleated, corner pleated, fringed, etc. View the chair as a series of rectangles, i.e. inside back; outside back; inside arm; outside arm; arm front; seat; front gusset; dust ruffle (valance); cushion pieces; armcover.

Measure the chair for each of these pieces, adding $1\frac{1}{4}$–$1\frac{1}{2}$ in (3–4 cm) seam allowance in each direction, plus 4–8 in (10–20 cm) for the "tuck-in". (Push your hand down into the chair around the seat and the inside arm to check the depth available for the tuck-in.) The tuck-in should be as large as the space allows. The farther the fabric cover can be pushed in, the less likely it is to pull out.

Seams should never be in the center of a cover. Always use a full width of fabric in the center with

seam positions

direction of pattern

panels joined to it at either side. Seams should always follow through from the front, across the seat and up the back (see diagram).

The pattern should be placed so that it is always the right way up (see diagram at the bottom of the previous page). The outside arm and the inside arm should never be cut as one piece for this reason. The pattern should match at each piping seam, and follow through from the floor, across the seat and up the back. Cushions should always be made to match the position of the pattern on the main body of the sofa or chair cover.

Plan these pieces on graph paper to make best use of the fabric width in estimating the amount needed. If you are using a patterned fabric, mark the graph paper into sections to show the repeat and the size of the pattern. Cushions should be planned so that the backs and fronts are the same, so that they will be individually reversible or reversible with each other. The shape of the sofa or chair will dictate the reversibility of the cushions. Sample cutting layouts are shown here and on the next page for an armchair, a sofa, and seat and shaped back cushions for a sofa.

Cutting

Covers are always cut for each chair individually. Although two chairs might look the same, they very rarely are. Covers must always be cut with the fabric pinned in place, right side out, as it will look when finished. This is because not only are two chairs never exactly the same, but neither are the left and right sides of any chair exactly the same! Label the cut pieces.

Cut out the pieces of fabric as planned on the estimate. Make up the piping cord for the whole job. Using the tape measure, carefully position a vertical row of pins to mark the center of the inside back, outside back, front and seat of the chair.

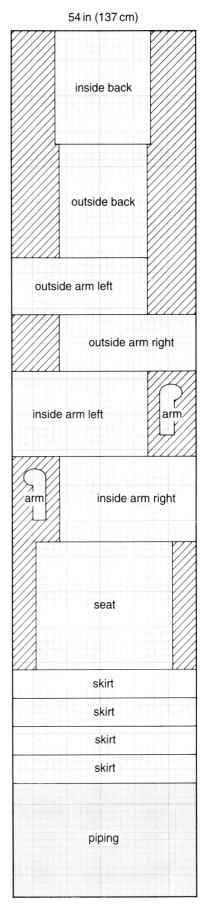

cutting layout – armchair

54 in (137 cm)

A	inside back	B
B	piping	A
A	outside back	B
B	piping	A

outside arm

outside arm

inside arm — arm / front

above: cutting layout – two or two-and-a-half seat sofa

54 in (137 cm)

arm / front — inside arm

seat

seat cushion top | seat cushion top

seat cushion bottom | seat cushion bottom

seat edge strip
seat edge strip
seat edge strip
seat edge strip
zipper edge strip
ruffled (frilled) skirt
ruffled (frilled) skirt
ruffled (frilled) skirt
ruffled (frilled) skirt
ruffled (frilled) skirt
ruffled (frilled) skirt
ruffled (frilled) skirt

*right: cutting layout – seat cushions and shaped back cushions
for a two or two-and-a-half seat sofa*

54 in (137 cm)

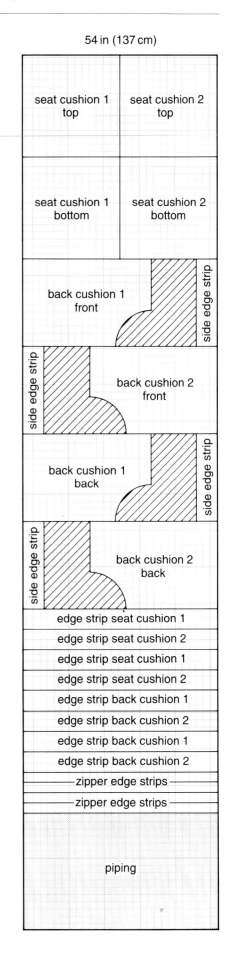

seat cushion 1 top | seat cushion 2 top

seat cushion 1 bottom | seat cushion 2 bottom

back cushion 1 front — side edge strip

side edge strip — back cushion 2 front

back cushion 1 back — side edge strip

side edge strip — back cushion 2 back

edge strip seat cushion 1
edge strip seat cushion 2
edge strip seat cushion 1
edge strip seat cushion 2
edge strip back cushion 1
edge strip back cushion 2
edge strip back cushion 1
edge strip back cushion 2
zipper edge strips
zipper edge strips

piping

SLIPCOVER (LOOSE COVER) FOR A DINING ROOM CHAIR

Materials

top fabric
muslin (calico) or plain cotton for
  pattern (optional)*
½ in (13 mm) wide tape for ties,
  approximately 6½ yds (6 m)
piping cord to go all around
fabric and piping for skirt as
  required

*If this is your first attempt at
making a slipcover, it is a good
idea to make up in muslin (calico)
first, then use this as a pattern for
the top fabric.

First Stage: Measuring and Pinning

1 Measure the chair at the widest
and highest points. Add 2½ in
(6 cm) all around for seam allowances.
Allow 6 in (15 cm) for the tuck-in at the
back of the seat, and 8 in (20 cm) for the
flap under the chair seat. Decide
whether you want to have a skirt around
the chair seat, and if so, the style and
fullness. Also consider whether to have
any other decoration, such as bows or
ties and allow extra fabric.

Plan these pieces on graph paper to
calculate the fabric needed – allow for:
front, back, seat, skirt, piping. Make
allowance for any pattern repeat and
choose the pattern position on the chair
back and seat.

2 Cut pieces of fabric as planned.
Measure all around and make up
enough piping (see page 18).

3 Measure across the back, front,
and seat of the chair and mark the
center lines with vertical rows of pins.
Fold the front and back pieces of fabric
in half lengthwise and finger press the
center line. (If the fabric is such that the

press line will mark it, measure and pin the center line.) Position these pieces, one at a time, with the right side of the fabric facing out, on the chair, pinning the fabric pieces to the center lines and anchoring in place at roughly 5 in (13 cm) intervals all around.

4 Holding the back and front pieces firmly between finger and thumb, pin together along the back edge of the chair. Start at the center top and pin around at roughly 6 in (15 cm) intervals. Pin back into these gaps, with the pins against the back edge to give a good stitching line. Pins should be nose to tail, giving a smooth line to follow.

5 Pin the top corners into a dart. Cut away excess fabric to leave a $\frac{3}{4}$ in (2 cm) seam allowance. Clip notches at irregular intervals. Make single, double, and triple cuts. These notches will be used to match the back to the front once the pins have been removed, so are vital for the cover to fit well. Make enough notches to make re-matching easy.

6 Unpin the top corners and fold the fabric inside toward the top of the chair. Clip into the seam allowance from the side so that the fabric tuck will lie flat. Using double thread, ladder stitch the foldline, finishing off with a triple stitch at the corner, on the seam allowance.

7 Place the seat piece on the chair seat, matching the center line and anchoring all around as before. Pin the fabric into a dart at the front corners.

8 Trim away the seam allowance to the dart. Pin the fabric to the lower edge of the chair seat all around. Make tailor tacks with contrasting thread to mark the junction of the leg with the seat and the front and back corners.

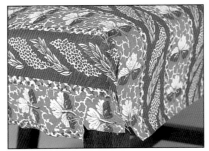

9 Cut away the fabric to leave a $\frac{3}{4}$ in (2 cm) seam allowance around the leg. Clip at an angle into the tack point. Repeat with the other front leg.

10 At the back of the seat, fold the front piece on itself, so that the foldline forms the eventual stitching points which will join the seat to this piece (at the corners). Make tailor tacks at $\frac{3}{4}$ in (2 cm) intervals along this line.

11 Push your hand into the chair to find the depth available for the tuck-in allowance. Cut away excess fabric, leaving a $\frac{3}{4}$ in (2 cm) seam allowance, from the chair back to the start of the tuck-in. Clip to the seamline at the innermost tack at the side to allow the fabric for the tuck-in to lie flat on the chair seat with the side seam allowance still folded up.

12 Fold the back of the seat back onto itself, so that the fold lines up with the fold of the front piece and joins the innermost tack. Clip across the folded seat piece toward the tack on the front piece, so that both cuts now meet at the seamline at the start of the tuck-in.

13 Pin the seat front to the chair back at each side. Fold the seat fabric down, from the cut to the chair back, so that the fold meets the folded seam allowance of the chair front. Make tailor tacks exactly opposite the others, so that they will match up accurately for stitching. Trim away excess fabric leaving the $\frac{3}{4}$ in (2 cm) seam allowance. Pin the chair front and seat pieces together to make the tuck-in, and cut from the front of the tuck-in piece to the back at an angle to allow the tuck-in to fit more easily.

14 Mark the back leg/seat join and cut away the back leg piece in the same way as the fronts in step 9. Measure 5–6 in (13–15 cm) down from the bottom of the seat. Cut away excess fabric, so that the flap to turn under is exactly the same depth all around.

15 Check that all seam allowances have been cut accurately and enough notches made. Remove all anchor pins and carefully take the cover off the chair.

Second Stage: Stitching

1 So that the whole cover is not unpinned at once, work on one section at a time. Unpin the seam between the seat and chair front on one side and enough of the back to front and along the tuck-in to allow you to work on this seam easily. Turn inside out. Match the tailor tacks. Pin along the seamline. Machine stitch two lines closely together to reinforce this seam. Do not be afraid to stitch close to the end of the easement cuts. The cover will fit accurately only if all marks are followed exactly, and unless these cuts are close to the seamline the join will pull. Repeat with the other seam. Undo the rest of the tuck-in, place right sides together, and machine stitch. Trim the seam allowances all around.

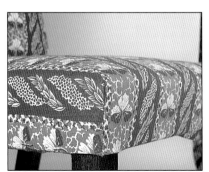

2 Baste (tack) the darts on the front of the seat, and unpin. Turn inside out and pin back together along the

basting (tack) lines. Machine stitch carefully, tapering the dart gradually. Trim the seam allowances. Press on the right side, using a damp cloth to give a good finish and a smooth line.

3 Unpin the back and front pieces. Pin the piping all around the back piece, on the seamline, cutting right up to the piping stitching line at the corner, and bending it tightly around the corner to produce a sharp edge (see page 18). Clip and ease where necessary. Machine stitch in place.

4 Pin the front to the back, matching the notches and the seamlines. Pin into the corner so that the corner cut opens out and the dart lies flat along the top. Pin the triple handstitch, made at step 6 of the pinning stage, so that it lies right on the seamline at the corner of the piping. Pin at right angles across the piping to ease any fullness around the top curve.

5 Machine stitch together. At the back leg position, trim the piping even with the bottom of the fabric. Pull $\frac{3}{4}$ in (2 cm) of the cord from the piping casing. Cut the cord and pull the casing back, so that the piping casing lies flat from the seamline to the bottom (see page 19).

6 Make a facing for each leg. Pin the corner of the leg onto a small piece of muslin (calico) and draw around. Remove the top fabric and cut the facing $2\frac{1}{2}$ in (6 cm) deep, following these lines. Repeat with the other legs. Pin to the top fabric, right sides together. Machine stitch around the inside edge. Press and fold under to the back, mitering the corners. Slipstitch to the chair cover as invisibly as possible.

7 Make a $\frac{3}{4}$ in (2 cm) double hem on all four flaps, leaving the ends open. Using a large blunted needle or a safety pin, thread the $\frac{1}{2}$ in (13 mm) tape through each of the pockets. To save pulling the tape out by mistake when you are working, attach a large safety pin to the other end, and thread through a continuous loop. Pull approximately 1 yd (1 m) of tape out at each corner and cut in the middle, so that each corner has two $\frac{1}{2}$ yd (50 cm) tapes to tie around the legs.

8 Press the cover thoroughly. Slip onto the chair, finger pressing seam allowances toward the back of the chair, and easing corners into position. Tie bows under the seat at each leg and tuck the tapes inside the flaps. Press cover again on the chair if necessary.

9 If you wish to have a skirt on the chair cover, make up as described on pages 143–5. Pin the piping all around the line of the bottom of the seat and machine stitch in place. You will probably be able to make up the skirt in one piece without a closure. If a closure is necessary, see page 142.

SLIPCOVER (LOOSE COVER) FOR A CHAIR OR SOFA

Materials

top fabric
muslin (calico) for pattern
  (optional)*
long-bladed, sharp scissors for
  cutting
short, sharp scissors for snipping
long pins
yardstick (meter rule)
tape measure
piping cord
½ in (13 mm) wide tape for
  holding corners
hooks for closure
pins and needles
matching and contrasting thread

*If this is your first attempt at
making a slipcover, it is a good
idea to make it up in muslin
(calico) first, then use this as a
pattern for the top fabric.

First Stage: Pinning

1 Find the center vertical line of the inside back of the chair using a tape measure, and mark with pins. Fold the inside back piece in half lengthwise, right sides together. Finger press lightly. Line up the foldline against the pinned center line and pin at top and bottom. Open out the piece and pin at 4–8 in (10–20 cm) intervals to anchor to the sides and top of the chair. Pins should be at right angles to the chair with the points inward. Repeat with the outside back, anchoring the fabric to the sides and bottom of the chair frame as well.

Holding the fabric firmly between finger and thumb, pin the pieces together along the back edge of the chair. Remember that the pin line will be the seamline/piping lines. The pins should be nose to tail, lying against the furniture to give an accurate line for stitching later. Start and finish 1½–2½ in (4–6 cm) above the arm on both sides. Pin from the back of the chair, and ease the front piece around any curves.

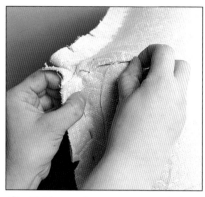

2 Fold over the top corner and pin. Cut away the excess fabric, leaving a ¾ in (2 cm) seam allowance. Cut notches into the seam allowance, so that the pieces can be easily re-matched for stitching. Unfold the top corner and pleat inward. Using a small needle and double thread, ladder stitch along the foldline with tiny stitches. Fasten off securely at the corner of the chair back. Clip carefully into this point from the top and side.

3 Position the inside and outside arm pieces of one arm on the chair, checking that the pattern is in the right place, and that the grain is straight vertically and horizontally. The pattern and grain of the outside arm should be level with the floor, not with the top of the arm. Pin these pieces together along the arm, making allowance for any arm curvature. The seam may be at the top of the arm, on the outside of the arm, or under the scroll, depending on the actual arm style of the chair. Repeat with the other arm.

4 Pin the arm front to the chair, checking that the grain is straight. Mark the position with two crossed pins. Anchor all around, with pins at right angles to the chair, points inward.

5 Pin the inside and outside arm pieces to the arm front, easing curves and fullness. Some arms will have no fullness to ease, other arms will need one or two darts at this point, but usually the excess fabric will be eased in with small gathers or pleats, spread evenly around the curved section. Trim away the excess fabric, leaving a ¾ in (2 cm) seam allowance.

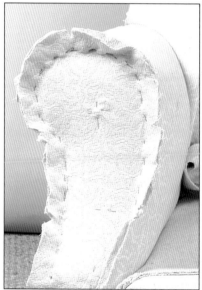

Cut notches all around for matching. Stitch individual tailor tacks in contrasting thread to each piece at the actual meeting point of the arm seam with the arm front, and at any other place where they might be useful for matching the pieces before stitching. Repeat with the other arm.

6 Pin the outside arm pieces to the chair outside back piece from just below the arm to the bottom of the chair. At the top of one arm, fold the inside back piece up so that the foldline marks the eventual stitching line along the top of the arm, which will start at the seat and go up around the arm to the back. Pin firmly to the inside back piece.

Check that there are no puckers under the folded back fabric which might be distorting this foldline. Fold the inside arm piece back on itself in the same way, so that these two pieces meet at the back.

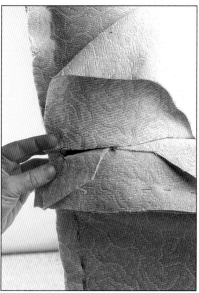

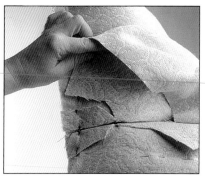

7 Pin the inside arm piece firmly to the inside back piece. (In some chairs, the inside arm will meet the outside arm at a point a little way along the arm toward the front. In this case pin this join first.) Trim away the excess fabric to 1¼–1½ in (3–4 cm) seam allowance as far as the start of the curve of the arm and the seat back (do not trim this too close yet in case some adjustment is needed). Stitch tailor tacks on two pieces 3 to 4 times along the folds at exactly opposite points, so that the pieces can be matched accurately for seaming. Use contrasting thread and secure stitches. You do not want to risk these marks pulling out.

8 At the top of the arm, from the previous cut line, carefully fold back the inside arm piece and the inside back piece along the curve of the inside arm. Trim away the excess fabric, marking the opposite points with tailor tacks as before.

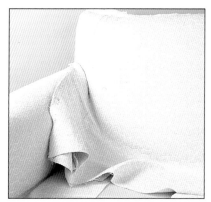

9 Clip into the seam allowance to allow the fabric to curve around the arm. Gradually cut the seam allowance back to ¾ in (2 cm). Take your time with this step, working with 1 in (2.5 cm) of fabric at a time around the curve, until you are happy with the

way the fabric is lying around the curve. Cut to the top of the inside of the arm and leave the fabric pinned back until the seat piece has been put in. Repeat with the other arm.

You might prefer to make a light pencil line along the folds if the chair has a difficult join, just to check that there aren't any unforeseen puckers or errors before you cut.

10 Place the seat piece on the chair seat, matching the center fold to the pinned line as for the two back pieces. Anchor all around, with pins pointing into the seat. Fold the two sides over along the lengths of the arms, so that the foldlines join the arm fronts at the edge of the front of the chair. Pin the front gusset to the front of the chair, checking that it is centered and level with the floor. Pin the top of this piece to the seat piece along the front edge. Where these two pieces meet the arm

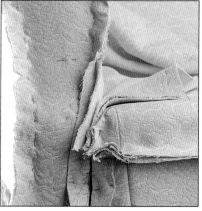

front, push a pin through all three pieces so that there is a definite point at which all pieces will meet when stitched. Mark each piece individually with a secure tailor tack in contrasting thread at this point.

11 Pin the front gusset to both arm fronts, from the marked join to the bottom of both pieces. Measure and mark the folded back sides of the seat piece so that the tuck-in is even from front to back along the length of the arm. Cut along this line.

12 Pin the inside arm pieces to the seat piece for about 8 in (20 cm) from the front toward the back, cutting back and shaping the join to correspond with the available tuck-in allowance. (Push your hand into the side of the seat to check where the tuck-in will start and how deep it is at each point.)

13 Measure and mark the tuck-in allowance with pins on the inside arm piece. Hold the inside arm piece and the inside back pieces

together and cut the tuck-in allowance so that both sides are equal and the tuck-in at the bottom matches the tuck-in allowed on the seat. (At first you might find this difficult; however, since this area is out of sight you can add in an extra section or make a gusset if you find this easier. Some arms are very hard to get absolutely perfect, and if all else fails a strategically placed cushion can cover an error.) Repeat with the other arm.

14 Using a 12 in (30 cm) ruler, measure up from the floor all around to the skirt position. Mark with pins. Add the seam allowance, then cut away the excess fabric. At this point, if

the cover needs to have a back opening, fold back the outside arm piece and the back piece to allow the necessary ease. Pin the fabric back on itself to keep the fold. Mark the top of the opening with a tailor tack on each piece.

15 Trim all seam allowances so that they are even. (If you have accidentally under-cut at any point, mark the place, so that you can adjust the seam allowance to compensate when pinning the pieces together.) Make sure that you have cut enough notches for matching. Use single, double and triple cuts to make matching easier. Remove the anchor pins and lift the cover off.

Second Stage: Stitching

If you want the cover to be loose, you will need to stitch so that the seam allowance is less than that allowed. (For example, a stitched seam allowance of $\frac{5}{8}$ in (1.5 cm) instead of the $\frac{3}{4}$ in (2 cm) allowed in cutting will give a $\frac{1}{8}$ in (0.5 cm) easement on each side of the seam. This would result in a loose cover.) Pin the piping so that the front of the cord is on the seamline to make a slightly loose cover. The

instructions below are for a tight cover with the stitching line of the piping pinned along the seamline. Make your own adjustments as you prefer, being consistent throughout the construction.

You will probably not be confident enough at this stage to take the whole cover apart and turn it all around, therefore work with small areas at a time, so that there is a limited amount of the unstitched cover unpinned at any one time.

1 Take the pins from one of the seams joining the inside arm to the back. These seams are probably the most vulnerable to movement and fraying so should be stitched and secured first. Turn inside out. Starting at the back, carefully match the tacks, and the ends of the easement cuts. Pin the seam down to the seat. Machine stitch, reinforcing the curve line by stitching two rows very close together. Do not be afraid to stitch right next to the cuts. If you give these too much slack the cover will not fit back as well as it came off. Trim the seam allowance. Repeat with the other side.

2 Next unpin one of the inside arm/ outside arm seams. If piping is to be used on the seam, pin the piping to the right side of the outside arm piece. Machine stitch in place. Pin the inside

arm to the piping line, right sides together, so that the seamlines and notches match. Pin along the piping line and at right angles to it. Machine stitch. Remove the pins along the piping as the machine approaches, but leave the others in place to prevent the two layers of fabric from moving apart. Stitch as close to the piping as possible. Check from the front that the previous stitching line is not visible.

If you have used piping, pull $\frac{3}{4}$ in (2 cm) of the cord from inside the casing at each end. Cut the cord away, so that the casing lies flat beyond the point at which the back and arm front seam will cross this one. Trim the seam. Repeat with the other arm.

3 Unpin the front gusset from the front seat. Turn inside out and pin the piping along the gusset piece.

Machine stitch. At the join with the arm front, pull the $\frac{3}{4}$ in (2 cm) of cord from the piping casing. Cut away the cord so that the case is flat beyond the tack mark. Pin the right side of the seat piece to the piping line, matching seam allowance and notches. Machine stitch the length of the piping, between the thread tacks. Secure stitches firmly at each end. Trim this seam.

4 One side at a time, unpin both sides of the seat from front to back. Turn inside out and pin together again, matching notches and seamlines. Machine stitch from the front tack mark to the seam at the back. Trim seams.

5 Unpin one of the front arms. Turn inside out. Pin piping all around the arm, to the right side of the fabric, clipping piping at $\frac{3}{8}$ in (1 cm) intervals to ease around curve. Make sure that you have pinned the piping to give a good shape. This is probably the first and most seen part of the chair. If the arm of the chair is not a good shape, you can adjust the shape of this piece slightly to improve the curve. Machine stitch the piping in place.

6 Pin the inside arm, outside arm, and the front gusset to the arm front, matching seamlines and notches. Pin the arm seam so that it is pressed downward. Ease any fullness carefully. Machine stitch from the bottom of the front gusset up to the join with the seat. Finish with the needle in the thread tack. Backstitch to secure. Lift the cover away from the machine. Fold over the seam and start again, with the needle in the tack mark, from the other side of the seam.

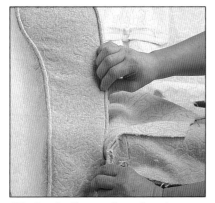

7 Stitch all around. Look at the stitching line from the front. You might find it quite difficult to get close to the piping the first time because of the joint difficulties of the curve and the fullness. Stitching a small section at a time, slowly stitch as close to the piping as you can, so that the previous stitching line is not visible from the front. Trim seam allowances. Repeat with other arm.

8 Unpin the back piece. Pin piping to the right side of the fabric, along both sides and across the top. At the top corners, clip into the piping to allow it to lie flat. Machine stitch in place.

9 Pin the front to the back piece along the piping line. Use plenty of pins, pinned at right angles to the

piping to ease any fullness. At the top corners make sure that the hand-stitched corners lie flat and that backstitching is within the seam allowance. Machine stitch in place, as close to the piping as possible, covering the previous stitching line. Stop the stitching at the top of the opening. Trim the seam allowances.

10 Slip the cover back onto the chair. Check that the seams are good. Re-stitch any problem areas.

11 To make a placket for the back opening, cut a piece of the top fabric $6\frac{1}{4}$ in (16 cm) wide and twice the length of the opening. Machine stitch the right side of this piece to the right side of the cover along the piping line on the back to the top of the opening. Turn the cover and stitch this piece along the seamline of the opposite side piece to the bottom of the cover. Press flat on the right side. Press this piece in thirds and fold toward the inside, so that the foldline encloses the seam. Handstitch to the stitching line. At the top of the opening, fold the placket in half and stitch across the width of the placket.

12 Pipe around the lower edge of the cover at the line previously marked for the skirt, with the piping line on the seamline (unless fitting a pie-crust ruffle/frill, see page 144). Machine stitch in place. At the back opening, pull $\frac{3}{4}$ in (2 cm) of the cord from the casing at each side and cut, allowing the casing to lie flat. Fold the casing over at a right angle at the end of the placket attached to the side piece, and at the piping edge of the back piece to neaten ends.

13 Make up the skirt as chosen (see pages 143–5).

14 Pin the skirt onto the piping line all around the chair cover, including the placket on the side piece, but finishing on the piping line of the back piece. If pleated, match the corners to the pleat openings; if gathered make sure the gathers are evenly distributed. Machine stitch in place. Trim the seam allowances. Fold the placket at the back over the seam and handstitch in place.

15 Lay the back opening on a flat surface, and mark positions at approximately 4 in (10 cm) intervals to stitch hooks and thread bars. Stitch one hook just inside the piping on the back and make a thread bar on the skirt at the other side to hold in place. Stitch the rest to marked positions.

16 Press all seams from the right side over a damp cloth. Press the cover and ease back onto the chair. Make sure that the seam allowances all lie in the same direction. Ease the cover around curves and corners. Finger press piping lines to straighten. You will need to spend time easing and fitting the cover in place on the chair to obtain the best fit. If you have made the cover tight, each seam will fit only as it was pinned and stitched so will need to be eased into that position.

17 Cut armcovers if wanted. Armcovers will be fitted, cut, and stitched in the same way as the main cover. Always fit over the finished cover and not on the chair itself. Allow approximately $\frac{1}{4}$ in (6 mm) ease all around for regular cleaning. The best armcovers are cut so that the fabric fits the whole length of the arm, down into the tuck-in on the inside arm, to the top of the skirt on the outside arm and to the back seam. Hand stitch a hem all the way around. Slipstitch the armcover to the chair cover along the back seam and along the top of the skirt.

To remove for cleaning, cut these stitches, then slipstitch back in position again afterward.

SLIPCOVER (LOOSE COVER) VARIATIONS

WING

To cut the wing, follow the same principles already used. After the outside and inside backs have been positioned and fitted across the top, pin the outside and inside wing pieces to the chair, keeping the grain straight. Pin to anchor all around. Ease the fullness around the wing shape, pinning from the back of the chair, to ensure that the pin line (and therefore the seamline) follows the shape of the chair exactly.

Fold back the fabric at the bottom of the wing where the wing piece will join the inside arm piece, following the shape dictated by the chair.

There are several different wing shapes, and the wing/back and wing/arm joins will vary with the chair style, so each will need to be assessed individually.

Follow the instructions for the folding back, cutting away, and tack marking processes described in steps 6 to 9 on pages 139–40 to fit the inside and outside arm pieces to the wing and the inside and outside back pieces to the inside and outside of the wing.

Make up the wing/inside back seam as step 1 of the stitching instructions. From this point, treat the wing as one with the chair back.

SKIRTS

Six different styles of skirt are described below. For each one, first decide the depth you wish it to be, then add seam allowances of $\frac{3}{4}$ in (2 cm) for the top and $1\frac{1}{4}$ in (3 cm) for the hem. Measure the sides, front, and back of the chair separately. Plan your skirt to fit the four sides. Each of the skirts described is lined, some with a contrasting color.

Ruffled (frilled)

Add the measurements of the four chair sides together and multiply by the fullness required – usually two to two-and-a-half times. Add 2 in (5 cm) for the overlap at the opening. Divide this figure by the width of the fabric, and cut the number of widths required to make this length.

Cut lining the same depth and enough widths for the same length.

Machine stitch the pieces together and press the seams flat. Pin the top fabric and lining together along one long side. Machine stitch $\frac{5}{8}$ in (1.5 cm) from the edge. Press the seam allowances toward the lining on the seam side. (If the top fabric is heavy, pressing the seam allowances toward the lining allows the main fabric to remain flat.)

Fold the skirt so that $\frac{3}{8}$ in (1 cm) of the top fabric is turned to the inside. Press. Pin the top edges together at 8 in (20 cm) intervals. Trim away any excess lining. Stitch a gathering thread $\frac{3}{4}$ in (2 cm) from the top edge. Divide the length of the skirt by 10. Measure this length all around the skirt and mark securely with pins along the top, so that there are ten divisions.

Divide the total measurement of the four chair

sides by 10. Using this figure measure around and mark the piping line into ten sections. Pin the skirt sections to the chair cover sections, right sides together, along the piping stitching line. Pull up the gathering threads and distribute the fullness evenly within each section. Pin at right angles to the piping, so that the pins can remain in place to hold gathers while machine stitching. Stitch all around as close to the piping as possible. Trim the seam allowances.

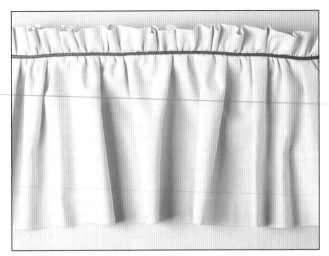

Bound ruffle (frill)

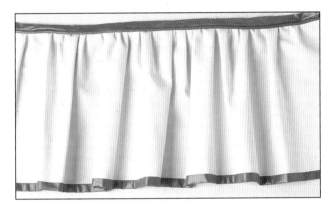

Calculate the length of ruffle (frill) required as above. Cut the top fabric the depth of the finished ruffle, plus $\frac{3}{4}$ in (2 cm) seam allowance for the top. Cut the contrast backing fabric the depth of the finished ruffle plus $\frac{3}{4}$ in (2 cm) seam allowance for the top and $1\frac{1}{2}$ in (4 cm) for the hem. Stitch the top fabric and the backing fabric right sides together, along the lower edge, $\frac{5}{8}$ in (1.5 cm) in from the edge. Press the seam allowances toward the backing fabric, so that the main fabric remains flat. Press the backing fabric under, leaving $\frac{2}{3}$ in (1.75 cm) showing on the front. Pin along the top edge to hold fabrics together, raw edges matching. Stitch a gathering thread $\frac{3}{4}$ in (2 cm) from the top. Pin to the cover and distribute fullness as described above.

Pie-crust ruffle (frill)
Measure all around the chair including the overlap at the opening and make up piping to this measurement. Do not stitch piping to the main cover. Make up one ruffle (frill) as above, to your

chosen depth and fullness. Make up a second shorter ruffle of approximately $1\frac{1}{2}$–$2\frac{1}{2}$ in (4–6 cm) finished depth and to the same fullness. Divide the lengths of piping and both ruffles by 10. Mark each piece into ten sections. Gather up the longer ruffle, and pin to the piping at each section, spreading the fullness equally between the sections. Machine stitch together. Place the shorter ruffle on top and machine stitch to the piping. Machine stitch this triple seam to the main cover. Trim the seam allowances and ends. Press the short ruffle upward to form a "pie-crust".

Butterfly ruffle (frill)

Decide the total depth of the ruffle (frill) to suit the chair and work out the fullness and widths of fabric needed as above. Cut the top fabric to exactly the depth of the finished ruffle. Cut the backing fabric to this depth plus $2\frac{3}{4}$ in (7 cm). Machine stitch the two pieces together, right sides together and raw edges matching, along the length of the fabrics, stitching the top line $\frac{9}{16}$ in (1.4 cm) in from the edge and the bottom line $\frac{3}{4}$ in (1.9 cm) in from the edge. Turn right side out. Press seam allowances toward the backing fabric. Trim the short sides. Stitch a gathering thread along the top edge approximately $1\frac{3}{8}$ in (3.5 cm) down. Divide the length by 10 and mark into sections. Divide the chair cover into ten equal sections. Pin the sections together so that the gathering thread is on the seamline. Pull up so that the fullness is distributed evenly. Machine stitch the ruffle to the cover with a small zigzag stitch to hold in place.

Corner pleated

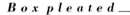

Measure each of the four chair sides. Add 16 in (40 cm) for each corner pleat, and $1\frac{3}{8}$ in (3.5 cm) for the overlap at the opening. Plan to cut each section so that there are no visible seams. (Sofas will still have the two seams at front and back either side of the central width.) It should be possible to place the seams so that they are hidden inside the pleats at each corner.

Cut the skirt to the required finished depth plus $1\frac{1}{2}$ in (4 cm) seam allowances. Seam as planned. Cut lining to match. Machine stitch the two lengths together along the lower edge $\frac{5}{8}$ in (1.5 cm) in from the edge. Press the seam allowances toward the lining, so that the main fabric is not folded. Fold so that $\frac{3}{8}$ in (1 cm) of the top fabric is turned to the inside and press. Pin the fabric and lining together. Handstitch the short ends to enclose the raw edges. On the right side, measure and mark out the chair front, back, and sides, and the corner pleats. Pin pleats in position. Baste (tack) pleats in place along the hemline. Press. Machine stitch to the piping line on the chair cover. Trim the seam allowances. Remove basting (tacking) stitches.

Box pleated

Measure each of the four chair sides. Multiply by three. Make up skirt as above. Lay the length of fabric on the worktable and plan the pleats so that a pleat breaks at each corner. Pin and tack pleats in place. Machine stitch to the cover along the piping lines. Press and trim seam allowances. Remove basting (tacking) stitches.

BENTWOOD CHAIR

An old wooden or metal bentwood chair can be given a new lease on life with this pretty cover.

Use for dressing tables, or as an occasional chair in a bathroom, or guest bedroom.

Materials

foam cut to the seat template
small piece of polyester batting (wadding)
top fabric as estimate
lining, same amount as top fabric plus an extra piece for the seat
½ in (13 mm) tape for ties, 12 in (30 cm) long × 4
½–1 in (13–25 mm) tape for binding the frame
piping cord

1 Measure the chair inside and outside backs, seat size, and skirt length. Make a template for the seat (see page 117). Plan the fabric cuts, allowing double fullness for the skirt and rectangles for the inside and outside back pieces, taking the widest and longest measurement plus 2½ in (6 cm) seam allowance. Bind the top, sides and seat back lightly with tape to give a soft area to pin into.

2 Cut the back pieces from the top fabric and lining as planned. If the top fabric is patterned, position the inside back and outside back considering where the most dominant part of the pattern should be. Place the lining and top fabric pieces with wrong sides together and baste (tack) together.

3 Fold each piece lightly in half lengthwise. Place the front piece, right side out, on the inside back, with the fold along the center of the chair. Pin to the tape at the top and bottom.

4 Holding the fabric firmly, but not pulling too hard, pin the back and

front together all around the back. You might need to pin roughly, then re-pin until you are happy with the result. The cover should be a good shape, but not too tight.

5 Trim away the excess fabric, leaving a ¾ in (2 cm) seam allowance all around. Cut notches in the

146

seam allowances to facilitate re-matching later. Trim the bottom edge to $\frac{3}{4}$ in (2 cm) lower than the seat.

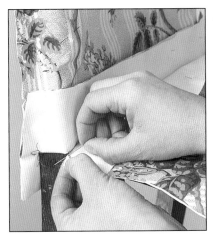

6 Cut the seat piece out of the top fabric, following the template and adding $1\frac{1}{4}$ in (3 cm) seam allowance all around. Place the foam slab onto the seat and place the fabric on top. Pin to the inside piece and shape around the legs if necessary. Mark any difficult joins with tailor tacks in contrasting thread. Mark the seamline all around where the fabric touches the seat.

7 Measure up from the floor to the seat at several points around the chair for the skirt length.

8 Make up enough piping (see page 18) to go once around the back of the chair and around the seat.

9 Unpin the back pieces. Pin the piping to the outside back all around, on the seamline. Clip into the seam allowance to enable the piping to lie flat. Machine stitch in place.

10 Pin the outside back to the inside back, matching notches and seamlines. Clip as necessary. Machine stitch all around as close to the piping cord as possible. Check from the front that none of the previous stitching line is visible. If it is, re-stitch closer to the cord and inside the last stitching line.

11 Unpin the seat/back section. Cut a piece of lining to the exact size of the seat piece. Place on the

worktable and press flat. Place the seat piece over it (right side up) and pin together at roughly 4 in (10 cm) intervals all around. Pin the piping around the outside edge, on the seamline, clipping as necessary to the stitching line to make the piping lie flat. Machine stitch in place.

12 Attach the inside back piece, matching the seamlines and any tailor tacks.

13 To make the skirt, cut widths of fabric to give at least double fullness, the length as measured plus $2\frac{3}{4}$ in (7 cm). Cut the lining to match. Machine stitch seams. Pin the fabrics together on the hemline, with the right sides together. Machine stitch around $\frac{5}{8}$ in (1.5 cm) in from the edge. Press seam allowances toward the lining from the back and from the front. Press the hemline, turning $\frac{5}{8}$ in (1.5 cm) of the top fabric toward the lining.

14 Pin the top edges together. Stitch two rows of gathering thread 1 in (2.5 cm) and $\frac{5}{8}$ in (1.5 cm) below the top.

15 Divide the length into eight equal sections and pull up the threads to gather the skirt. Divide the seat top into eight equal sections and mark with pins. Pin the section markers together and gather the skirt into the sections. Distribute the gathers evenly.

16 Pin together along the piping line and at right angles to the piping to keep gathers straight. Machine stitch close to the piping. Machine stitch around again from the seat side, inside the previous stitching line, to ensure a neat finish. Make a

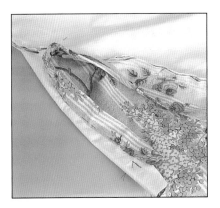

placket for the side opening (see page 142, step 11).

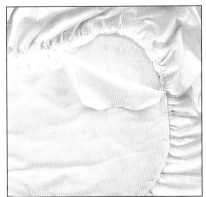

17 Trim all seam allowances. Turn the cover right side out and press. Cover the top of the foam pad with batting (wadding) and place on the inside of the seat, against the lining and under the seams. Pin the extra piece of lining on top and turn under the raw edges all around. Handstitch to enclose the foam pad.

18 Fit the cover back onto the chair, finger pressing the seam allowances toward the back and making an even piping line around the back. Position the seat pad and pull the skirt into place.

ALL-IN-ONE COVER

A useful, informal cover can be made to cover any sofa with just a large square of fabric which has ties stitched at the front and back corners to hold the cover in place. A large reversible rug or blanket could be used instead of fabric, especially for a child's bedroom or playroom. Choose one which is easy to clean.

All-in-one covers can be temporary arrangements for a new sofa to protect the top cover or to make a more attractive cover for a sofa awaiting re-upholstery. A slightly more sophisticated version can be made for long-term use with just a little fitting around the arms. Gussets of another fabric at the corners can be an attractive feature, with contrasting ties. Summer covers in a white cotton with blue ties and blue floral or checked inserts can make a refreshing room change – bright, stylish, and easy to launder.

The cover shown is a large rectangle using an all-over pattern for one side bordered with a co-ordinating fabric and a simple ticking stripe for the reverse, tied with fabric ties.

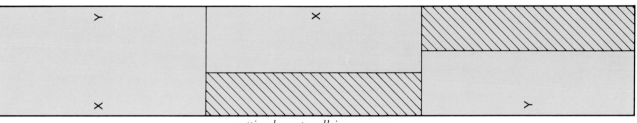

cutting layout – all-in-one cover

Materials

top fabric
lining fabric, same amount as top
    fabric
1 in (2.5 cm) grosgrain ribbon or
    extra fabric for ties
lightweight polyester batting
    (wadding) for quilting, if wanted
½ in (13 mm) tapes to tie cover
    underneath

---

1 Measure the sofa or chair to be
covered (see diagram): (a) from the
floor to the back, up over the back and
down to the seat, along the seat and
down to the floor at the front; (b) from
the floor at one arm, up over the arm,
down to the seat, along the sofa, over
the opposite arm to the floor.

Plan the fabric as required, so that
there is a full width of fabric at the
center with panels (parts of full widths)
seamed to either side.

2 Cut out both top and lining fabrics.
Machine stitch seams as planned.
Press flat.

3 Place the lining fabric right side
down on the worktable. Clamp at
the sides to hold it flat. Place the top
fabric over it, wrong sides together,
matching all seams. Hand stitch the
seam selvages together to prevent the
two fabrics moving independently on
the finished cover.

4 If using grosgrain binding, finger
press in half and pin all around the
two fabrics, lining up the raw edges with
the center foldline. Machine stitch all
around, making sure that both top and
lining are caught.

5 If using fabric binding, cut strips
2½ in (6 cm) wide and join to the
required length. Pin all around, right
sides together, lining up the edge of the
binding strips with the raw edges of the
other two fabrics. Stitch ⅝ in (1.5 cm)

from the edge. Press from the right side
and fold under to the back. Pin. Turn
cover over and fold the binding in half
again. Slipstitch all around, stitching
into the previous stitching line.

6 Put this cover over the sofa,
tucking into the seat back enough
so that the front and back just touch the
floor. Arrange the fronts and backs of
both arms, so that the folds are like
large pleats.

7 Stitch ½ in (13 mm) tapes, long
enough to tie under the sofa to hold
the cover in place, at three points along
the front and back on the seam and at
two points along each side.

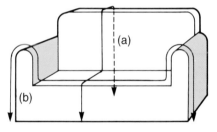

Quilting

If you would prefer to quilt this cover, add a layer of
batting (wadding) between the lining and the top
fabric at step 3. Pin the three layers together all
around the outside and along the seams. Mark the
quilt into 8–12 in (20–30 cm) squares. Baste (tack)
to hold all layers completely together. Quilt by
hand with a small running stitch or by machine
using a special "walking" foot along the basting
(tack) lines. Proceed from step 4.

Choosing Fabrics and Finishes

CHOOSING FABRICS

*M*ost upholstery fabrics are woven textiles. To be able to choose and use these fabrics successfully, you must understand something of the nature of the fibers and the method used to weave them. In other words, fabrics must be understood on a practical level as well as on a purely visual level. There are no "golden rules" to follow other than that the fabric must suit the purpose for which it is intended. This must be the first consideration, even before the color scheme is taken into account.

The structure of woven textiles is a combination of three elements:

1 The type and quality of raw materials used.
2 The structure of the weave.
3 The finish.

The type of raw material will have the greatest importance in suiting the fabric to its function. Check your chosen fabric against the following list:

Cotton
Natural cellulose extracted from seed head pods after plants have flowered; loses strength in sunlight (do not leave exposed to strong sun for long periods); fibers are stronger when wet than dry; shrinks unless pre-shrunk; soft to touch, but still strong; good moisture absorption; dries easily; easily laundered; very versatile – can be woven, knitted, etc; mixes well with almost all other fibers.

Linen
Made from the fibers inside the stalks of the flax plant; creases easily; very strong, both wet and dry; very absorbent; takes high temperatures; used to mix with other fibers to add strength; expensive, therefore often mixed with less expensive fiber; dyes do not always penetrate to inner core of threads, therefore colors can fade; attractive because yarn is uneven; very easy to work with and versatile.

Wool
Natural fiber from animals' coats; liable to excessive shrinkage as the "scales" on each fiber overlap easily and cause the fabric to harden and "felt" in warm water; expensive, so often blended to reduce the price; repels damp initially, although once the fibers are penetrated it is very absorbent; warm to touch; very springy, so not suitable for some uses.

Silk
Natural fiber usually from the cocoon of the silk worm fed on mulberry leaves – the coarser silks, wild silk, and tussah are made from worms whose diet is oak leaves; easy to dye but will fade in sunlight; soft, luxurious to touch; expensive, so sometimes mixed with cotton; mixes well with wool; strong fibers giving good elasticity and resilience.

Acrylic
Man-made from hydrocarbons;
fibers are not strong;
low elasticity;
little absorbency;
warm to the touch;
can be heat set, e.g. into permanent
pleats;
does not shrink once fully processed;
mixes well with wool and with cotton.

Rayon (Viscose)
Made from wood pulp or animal
waste;
fibers are weak and very absorbent – at
their weakest when wet;
liable to shrinkage;
mixes well with natural fibers;
washes well – sheds dirt easily;
easy to dye;
inexpensive.

The weave of the fabric will also be a
determining factor in your choice.
Fabric is woven on the loom with the
vertical "warp" threads fixed in place
and the horizontal weft threads worked
across, over and under the warp
threads, to produce a variety of weaves.
The warp is the stronger, thicker thread.

WEAVES

Plain Weave:
Weft is woven over one warp thread and
under the next. Tight and firm. Weight
determined by the diameter of the
threads.

Basket Weave:
Weft is woven over two, under two.
Produces a looser weave with more
drape. Strong.

Satin Weave:
Weft floats over 2 + warp threads and
under one. Gives a slight sheen. Very
hard-wearing.

Jacquard Weave:
The design of the finished cloth is
woven into the threads. Machine-made,
originally using a punchcard system
(now computerized) to form a reversible
pattern, using variations of weaving
techniques. Slow process, therefore
expensive.

Dobby Weave:
This is a simple, geometric pattern
(usually some form of "spot") made by
putting an attachment ("dobby") to the
loom to form patterns by leaving out
warp threads in a regular pattern.

Herringbone:
This is a broken satin weave, producing
vertical stripes.

Chevron:
Another twill weave which is broken to
form zigzags in a vertical line. Two or
more colors (or tones of one color) are
often used to emphasize the effect.

FINISHES

Finally, check the finish of the fabric, especially
the flameproofing. In the U.K. a flame-retardant
treatment is now required by law for all upholstery
and loose covers on post-1953 furniture. If the top
cover has not been treated, a fire-retardant barrier
cloth will need to be upholstered onto the piece of
furniture before the top cover.

Many cotton fabrics are "glazed" by applying
glue and shellac or starch to the surface after
printing, then ironing under pressure. Fabrics can
be heavily or lightly glazed, and will vary with the
manufacturer's preference. This gives an attractive
sheen and a high resistance to dirt penetration. The
glazed surface will wear away after a time and with
washing. It is not possible to re-glaze made-up
fabric, although stain repellency can be restored by
spraying with a product made for that purpose.

If the fabric you have chosen for its color does
not possess the right properties for the proposed
use, either discard it or change the rest of the
scheme to suit. For instance, it may be that you
have picked out an elaborate silk for your sofa and
then you find it is suitable only for draperies or
light upholstery. You may decide either to use the
proposed curtain fabric for the sofa, if suitable, and
use the silk for draperies, or to choose an
alternative sofa fabric in a plain color or a small
design, and use the silk for a smaller project, such
as chair back cushions, or to cover side chairs, or
as a tablecloth, so that this fabric still remains
important in the room. This is a method I often use
to complete a room within a given budget, as the
elaborate silk will almost always be more expensive
than a plain woven alternative.

CHOOSING COLORS

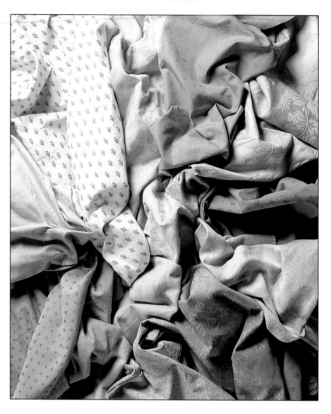

Green is the color of nature and all tones and hues of green will live happily together. Similarly, in the garden, other colors are viewed against a green background and this principle can be brought into the house. Use light tones of green for bedrooms, mid tones for sitting rooms, and deep rich tones for studies and book rooms.

Blues are often considered to be cold but the only cold blues are the icy turquoise tones, which can easily be avoided in favor of the deeper toned blue-cream, blue-green, and blue-yellow mixes of jacquard and damask weaves. For a fresh, summery room, use blues the color of Mediterranean seas and skies in simple cotton prints, stripes, and checks.

T he choice of color and style will be limited to a degree by the character of the house, by the style of furnishings already in the room, and by your own character, wishes, and family requirements. The choice is almost never isolated to the piece of furniture to be covered.

Reactions to particular colors are subjective and can profoundly affect the way we feel about ourselves, and about our environment, both inside and outside. It is, therefore, absolutely vital that you choose fabrics within the color spectrum with which you feel instinctively comfortable. This does not mean that the whole house will look the same, but it does mean that there will be a continuity from room to room and a color which will run

through the house in varying tones and intensity. Neither does this mean that you should keep to the same colors and tones for every room. This would be a recipe for complete boredom. Rather, you should identify the depths of colors with which you feel comfortable, then choose your fabrics and wall colors within this range but with a variety of solid colors, checks, stripes, weaves, and prints, so that they work together throughout the house. Stronger or bolder colors can always be introduced through edgings and trimmings to add highlights without overwhelming the overall scheme. These embellishments are described on pages 164 to 7.

Fabrics of similar weight, surface texture, tonal value, and richness work together best.

Red in its richest tones has always been the color of royalty. These intense tones are usually avoided in furnishings in favor of the browner, earthy tones and soft, dusty pinks. Deeper tones can be used in studies and dining rooms, and as a good background for paintings, while the softer pinks are popular choices for sitting rooms and bedrooms.

Yellow is the color of summer and is always warm and welcoming. Use mixed tones of ocher, gold, lemon, and buttercup, adding off-whites and creams to produce a gentle, comfortable decorative style. The deeper ochers and golds are a good foil for strong reds and greens; the sharper lemons and buttercups for summer blues and spring greens.

Monochromatic schemes, in which the texture, tone, and weight of the basic color are varied, prove comfortable, undemanding, and interesting. This is the safest way to begin a room scheme.

Add another color, either near in tone (related) or opposite (complementary), in a solid color or a small printed design, to add depth and interest, then bring in a small amount of a third, and possibly fourth, color.

The introduction of books, floor rugs, and paintings to the room instantly adds many colors which will lift the basic scheme as much or as little as you choose. If you want to make the room more informal, or comfortable, add mixed colorings. If you wish to keep the room stark, modern, or

monochromatic, add paintings and rugs which are in the same basic colors as the room scheme but which add an interesting textural dimension to otherwise flat surfaces.

If you are choosing the covering for just one item of furniture, as is often the case, try to collect pieces of all the other fabrics in the room as well as swatches of the wall and floor coverings, so that you can build up your own "color board" by sticking them onto a piece of cardboard, in direct proportion to their value in the room. Carry this with you when looking for fabrics. The type of floor covering and wall finish will have determined the main color and the atmosphere of the room. Texture is now the most important consideration – should the fabrics

Neutral colors can always be added to any color scheme but often work best on their own. With such a rich variety of tones, weaves, and textures available, a luxurious atmosphere can be created simply by the interplay of light on the fabrics. Mix together as many silks, linens, wools, cottons, designs, and weaves as you wish.

A scheme for a study. The starting point was the deep, earthy red of the walls. Wool curtains in a rich plaid, whose background color toned with the walls, allowed upholstery in a two-toned green, textured weave, a printed paisley, and a jacquard print, which introduced touches of ocher and blue. Shiny red silk cushions added a textural contrast.

be simple weaves, flat, embossed, shiny, heavy, light, floaty or dense?

The range of available fabrics is tremendous. Putting a variety of patterns and styles together in one room demands skill, knowledge of fabrics, textures and how they relate to each other, knowledge of the inherent fibers and the tonal values of color mixtures – but above all, and for which there is no substitute, a great deal of time and careful thought. If you find the choice difficult, ask the advice of a professional designer. Good decorators are happy to advise and supply you with your chosen fabric without having to take on the whole project. They will usually charge a small fee for their expertise, but will give you access to a

wide variety of fabrics and could save you from an expensive error.

If you have decided not to ask for professional help, use the many home magazines now available. They are full of ideas for room schemes, the latest fabrics and accessories available, and sometimes a mail-order fabric service. You will obviously not receive personal attention, but the advice given by writers and the ideas gathered from others' homes will be informative and helpful. It is often more important in the first instance to determine the "look" that you do *not* want before finalizing the one that you do.

Do not try to match the colors of different types of fabric exactly, since the weave of a fabric and the

A summer scheme. Two pretty cottons with a rose design in tones of blue and of green used with a variety of checks in both colors are used to cover sofas, chairs, and cushions. They are matched with off-white curtains giving a light and fresh room design. This is a good solution for summer chair covers as a change from the deeper-toned upholstery underneath.

A scheme for a low-ceilinged, farmhouse sitting room. Here the soft ocher walls gave the right background for upholstery fabrics in earth reds, golds, and tans, accented with the lovely, soft blue-greens in two of the fabrics. The basic weaving styles of checks, stripes, and spots maintain the simplicity of the scheme.

fiber content influence the way a color will appear. For example, a cotton and a silk dyed in the same color vat will absorb different densities of color. Also the amount and quality of the light within a room at any one time, throughout the day and throughout the seasons, vary tremendously, which will affect the tone and priority of the colors in the fabrics. Likewise if you change the position of a fabric within the room, you will alter the way the color of the fabric is perceived.

Always try a large piece of your chosen fabric in the room over a period of several days before making your final choice. Look at it in both dull and sunny weather if possible, at night, at dusk, and in the early morning. Consider which time of

day and year the room is most used and bear in mind that this is the priority time for the fabrics to work. For instance, you may use your dining room mainly in the winter months, preferring to eat outdoors or more informally in the summer months. You will find that there are rooms you prefer to sit in in the mornings and others which you really use only at night.

In the following pages fabrics have been grouped into six different types covering design, color, texture, and content. A selection of the fabrics available in each type is illustrated and the text discusses their advantages and disadvantages for upholstery. Details of the fabrics themselves are listed on pages 188–9.

SMALL MOTIFS

A motif is an isolated design visible against a plain or almost plain background. The motif may be woven or printed. A woven motif in a dobby weave (see page 153) may be self-colored on a plain fabric or picked out in one of the colors of a two-color fabric. Alternatively, motifs can be formed by changing the warp thread, carrying the extra threads behind the main fabric, bringing them forward to the surface when needed.

Printed motifs can be in a variety of colors. A lighter motif against a darker background is practical and has the advantage of relieving what would otherwise be a solid mass of color and perhaps too demanding or domineering in the room. A darker woven motif on a lighter background has the disadvantage, even with yellow or white, that the darker threads behind the cloth show through, creating a dark, shadow line between the motifs.

Small motifs, trellises, and geometric patterns define the shape of the piece of upholstery, and are useful for situations, such as dining chair seats, where cleaning or washing is difficult and marks are disguised by the pattern. Small motifs can be used on large sofas, and give a good background for scatter pillows (cushions) in mixes of patterned chintz and woven textiles. Fabrics with small motifs in tones of the main color rather than in a strong contrast color are arguably the most versatile and useful upholstery fabrics available.

STRIPES AND CHECKS

S triped and checked fabrics can be either utilitarian in nature or very stylish and elegant. They can be soft and muted or strong and dramatic.

Ticking (see page 187) may be used in neutral, contemporary room schemes or to upholster traditional furniture. Use tickings also for hidden areas – to line the inside of boxes, trunks, curtains, valances, etc.

Cotton, being a heavy yarn and capable of being tightly woven, can make good solid damasks which do not have the shine and richness of silk and silk/cotton mixes but which are durable and well suited to country-style rooms. Elegant and formal stripes and checks can be created using exactly the same designs as the utilitarian weaves, simply by changing the fiber content and depth of weave. Silks and wools have their own inherent qualities which give a richness to the weave, allowing light to be reflected in a quite different way from plain woven cotton. A moiré (watermarked) finish over rayon (viscose), silk or cotton cloth transforms a simple check, reflecting light in many directions to

give a rich, luxurious feel.

It is not usual to decorate a whole room in checks and stripes, using heavy weaves, if it is to be sophisticated and formal. However, stripes are often used for such rooms on a major area, such as walls, draperies, or large sofas. A formal chair, such as a high-backed French bergère, almost always looks best in a striped fabric.

Use stripes and checks to "fill-in", for example as footstool covers, for side chairs and dining chairs, window seat cushions, bed dust ruffles (valances), and headboards, for rooms which are otherwise full of patterned fabrics or plain colors.

Use stripes to change the appearance of a piece of upholstered furniture. Large stripes will make a piece of furniture (or a room) appear smaller, while narrow, fine stripes pick up the detail (especially on chairs with beautiful marquetry work) and can be used to exaggerate height.

Checks almost always look better flat – certainly only the simplest checks should be used for curtains – so are ideal for upholstery.

PRINTED COTTONS

Cotton used for upholstery relies for its decorative effect on the printed colors rather than on the depth of color, texture, and shading of a heavier woven cloth.

Floral chintzes were originally based on the Chinese designs of birds and flowers, and the tree of life from India, brought back from the East by the trading merchants. They have since been adapted to include every sort of flora and fauna, and now incorporate anything from King Charles spaniels to Minton tea cups.

French provincial prints descended from the small, geometric designs (called Les Indiennes) brought to France from India. These are block-printed by hand in strong, earthy colors.

Toile de Jouy encapsulated the essence of the era in which it was first printed. The copper rollers were engraved with idyllic pastoral scenes, which were then printed in one color onto a base cloth of muslin (calico).

Small patterns in one color on a plain background are extremely useful for small pieces of upholstery which "fill in" the details of a room scheme. Use them on side chairs, small armchairs, cushions, for example, in the sitting room and bedroom particularly.

Printed cottons are not very practical as coverings for sofas, because cotton will crease across the cushions and will soon look crumpled, and because cotton can be torn easily by buckles, etc. It does not have the "give" that a textured, woven cloth has. Another disadvantage of a printed fabric is that because the colors have been added to the surface of the cloth, they may not completely penetrate the threads and therefore will wear away with time.

Check that the repeat of the pattern and the elements which make up the pattern are in proportion to the size of the chair.

Check that the pattern is on-grain. Patterns which are not printed straight will require much more pulling to even them up with the sides of the chair or sofa. This not only takes more time, but also weakens the fabric. Also check fabric for printing flaws which could come just in the wrong place (see page 19).

RICH COLORS AND TEXTURES

Warm, rich colors can be used in a room which is naturally dark, with old yellows and ochers in spot colors included in the scheme to give the dark tones a "lift".

A living room or dining room with a northerly aspect, for example, will benefit from the natural warmth and depth of rich colors and pronounced textures. The addition of richly-patterned and woven textiles in dark corals and terracottas to a room decorated, for instance, with deep yellow walls will give a depth, weight, and character that no pale colors can.

Studies, family rooms, and libraries benefit from having a mixture of fabrics in patterns of varying scale and woven textures in rich colors. Time needs to be spent carefully balancing the scale of designs and the ratio of multi-colored pattern to self pattern in order to achieve a harmonious result, but colors can be kept very close together, relying on the weaves to give the interest.

Choose trimmings to add richness of fiber. Wool, silk, and linen braids and fringes work well with tapestry, wool damasks, shot silks, jacquard-woven textiles, bouclés, brocades, and velvets.

Keep the same weight of color throughout the room. Never use rich fabrics with a light floor unless it is to be covered with a large Persian rug. Polished wood floors add their own unique dimension and depth of color to rich fabrics, but will need rugs also. Wall colors should go with the main fabric colors and should not contrast greatly with any of the other furnishings.

SELF-PATTERNED FABRICS

Self-patterned fabrics are extremely successful used as mixer fabrics for multi-colored weaves and printed textiles. They both draw together and complement the main fabrics. An enormous variety of self-patterned and woven designs is available in thousands of colors in every hue and tone, so it should be simple to match one of the colors in the other printed fabrics in the room.

Floaty taffetas and silks, plain cottons, lightweight woven damasks, and jacquards in summer colors complement each other perfectly, incorporating a variety of weights and textures, but still retaining an airiness.

Bright, summery colors can be used together in a sunny, light room. Choose a main color which will "hold" all the other colors used, and which will be as comfortable in winter as in summer, and use this on the walls. Add furnishing fabrics in a mixture of solids and self patterns chosen carefully to keep the tonal balance.

Furniture can be covered in deeper colors but consider making slipcovers in stripes, checks, or small patterns to fit over the furniture to give a welcome decorative change for the summer. Cushions may be changed to suit the seasons – perhaps add blue and white simple prints for the summer and deeper tones and textured, woven fabrics for the winter.

SOFT-TONED FABRICS

*M*any people like to decorate their living rooms in soft, restful tones and colors, the most popular being soft dusky pinks with gentle greens turning either slightly to blue (aqua) or to yellow (pale olive).

Hand-printed designs, particularly on linen, lend a "powdery", faded appearance to the colors which gives a period look to a room. These fabrics are especially useful in a large room with heavy wood beams or paneling and antique furniture, or in any situation where bright modern colors would not complement the natural characteristics of the

room. Antique textiles are naturally becoming rarer all the time, so these hand-printed linens and cottons are good alternatives. They also have the advantage that the ground cloth is usually of the best quality and therefore the fabrics will wear extremely well.

Mix patterns of differing intensities and scale with small self-patterned fabrics and muted self weaves. Large areas of plain color in any tone will jar with the soft, gentle atmosphere produced by items of furniture upholstered in complementary, muted patterns.

TRIMMINGS

*O*nce the upholstery fabric has been chosen for its appropriate color and style, attention to the detail of the finish will make the piece individual and will determine how that piece will fit into the particular room scheme. Careful consideration will need to be given to the demands and restrictions of the piece to be upholstered. Is it traditional or contemporary? Does the line need to be emphasized or disguised? Will the cover be upholstered or loose? Do you want the chair to stand out in the room or to fit back in as though it had not been newly re-covered? Is the chair of good proportions generally —will it need a skirt to cover ugly legs or is the seat too high to take a skirt? The style of trimming will be dictated initially by the requirements of the chair, then the room.

To take the first point, a wood frame chair, such

as this Victorian lady's balloon back, will need to have a trimming which will cover up the upholstery tacks used to fit the cover in place. The braid will need to be wide enough to cover the tacks completely, and pliable enough to bend around the curves. The four most suitable finishes are:

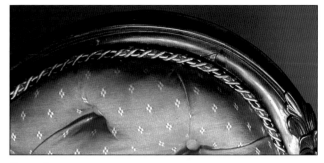

1 cord

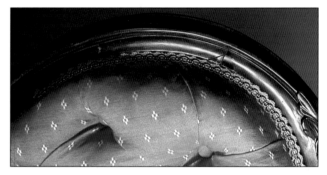

2 gimp

3 fan edging

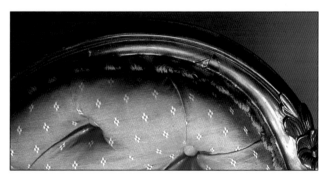

4 double piping

Which of these styles to use will be decided by personal preference, bearing in mind the other furnishings with which it will be placed.

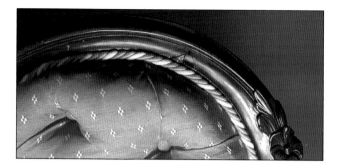

The room style will also be a major factor in the choice of color for the chosen trimming. Should the edging be immediately visible, slightly visible, or as invisible as possible? A strongly contrasting trimming will accentuate the shape of the piece and make a strong statement in the room. The chair will demand to be noticed.

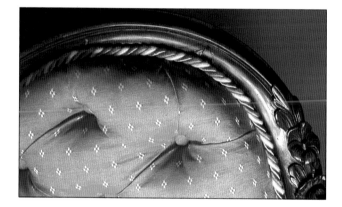

A softer contrast can pick up other colors in the room but be less obvious. When choosing a contrast color, keep the tonal qualities of the two colors as close as possible.

A trimming which has the color of the upholstery fabric plus one or two other colors will be noticeable but will be soft and will blend into the chair.

If the chair is not to be accentuated and the lines not to be emphasized, a trimming exactly matching the main fabric needs to be chosen.

Generally speaking, contemporary-style rooms can take strongly contrasting finishes, while traditionally furnished rooms require the chair to blend into the whole and so a near tone or muted, mixed colors are advised.

This upholstered table is part of a scheme using all natural fabrics in neutral colors. Throughout the whole scheme the contrast of black with the creams and off-whites has served to identify shapes.

To a certain extent the choice of a particular trimming is governed by budget, because there are small companies which are able to make any trimming in any color mix at any price. You may also be able to find antique trimmings with hand-sewn tassels from specialist antique fabric dealers, or by spending hours searching the antique markets. There is now, however, a large selection of ready-made trimmings from the traditional French *passementerie* houses and from small companies which produce their own ranges of cords, fringes, tassels, and braids, in every country.

PIPING

Piping is used to define the lines of the piece of furniture. The choice of color will depend on the formality of the piece and the atmosphere of the situation in which it will be placed. A strongly contrasting piping will suit straight, clean lines, and give a formal appearance.

Self piping is always used for an informal finish, for chairs and sofas of awkward shape, for lumpy arms and backs. The self-piped line will define the seamlines without drawing attention to the outlines of the chair.

A toning piping will identify the line without drawing attention to the finish at the expense of the rest of the piece.

If you are making a slipcover (loose cover), the piping will be placed along the pinned line and stitched in position. It will then provide a ridge to stitch the other piece of fabric against, so making it much easier to achieve straight seams. It is also much easier to sew a ruffle (frill) against a piped line than to a seam allowance.

Strongly contrasting piping demands that the seams be absolutely straight, so beginners should avoid it!

Loosely fitted covers will have some seams which will move around with use, so these should not be emphasized with piping.

CORD

Cord may be used as an alternative to fabric piping, again either in a contrast color to identify the line or in a matching color to blend in with the overall fabric. It is available in diameters of $\frac{1}{8}$ to $\frac{3}{4}$ in (3–20 mm), so you will be able to choose the most suitable size for your piece of furniture.

Cord may be stitched to upholstered furniture after the chair has been completely upholstered or, if flanged, it can be stitched into covers during the making up, in place of piping.

*F*INISHING *T*OUCHES

BOWS

Bows add a feminine touch to furnishings and can be great fun to make and use. Bows should be used only when the situation is right, and then they can be made a major feature. They should always be over-done and overstated rather than under-done. Make large bows; small ones look insignificant.

Pin bows to the backs of dining chairs with ruffled (frilled) skirts for a pretty look, or make up large bows to pin to the back of an otherwise minimal and austere chair for a daring contrast. The bows on the chair opposite have been made as small as possible in relation to the size of the chair, since the layout of the room afforded little space around the chair, but the tails have been left long to compensate. Use bows to tie cushions to the legs of dining and bedroom chairs for a decorative finish.

BUTTONS AND TUFTS

Buttons are used to emphasize shape, whether on a window or chair seat cushion, or at the back of a small chair. The decision about whether to use large or small buttons, buttons or tufts, contrasting or harmonious colors, is again one related to the style of the furniture, the style of the room and personal preference.

BUTTERFLY EDGING

This very pretty edging is simple but time-consuming to make. Its effect is to give a charming and individual edge to feminine treatments as on the dressing table on page 110, for example.

167

CONTEMPORARY STYLE

OUTDOOR ROOM

*T*his outdoor room has been transformed from a pile of bricks into a useful summer eating area with a built-in fireplace for outdoor cooking and for extra warmth on cool evenings. A simple stencil of hops, around the fireplace wall, and a random leaf and bird pattern on the other walls echo the colors of the clematis and climbing roses which fall around the front of the room. Paint rubbed into the window frames takes away any starkness, and the walls have been "aged" with a water wash finish.

The chairs and seats are an informal collection of mixed canes which can be left out through the winter with little maintenance. Cushions covered in stripes and a basket of flowers design in typically French provincial colors increase the Mediterranean feeling on a summer's day. These cushions are all designed to be simple to make and easy to remove for laundering. The chairs could be junk shop finds with the original paintwork left intact, the only changes being a re-upholstered seat and new cushion pad and cover. Instructions for making these pieces are given on pages 124–7.

TOWNHOUSE ROOM

*T*he decorating challenge for this townhouse room was to keep the furnishing colors light and to allow as much of the naturally available light as possible into the room. Fine roller shades (blinds) at each window fit right inside the cornice (pelmet) and can be pulled down to prevent glare when necessary and to allow privacy without blocking the daylight. The window drapes were chosen in the same color tones as the upholstery to give a unity and airiness to the room.

The two sofas are covered in an elegant woven damask stripe with a complementary plain damask for the curtains and for the chaise ottoman, which is used for extra storage and emergency seating. A colorful, hand-stitched rug gives a weight to the room and balances the painted leather screen on the wall. Pretty chintz pillows (cushions) add informality to the seating.

KITCHEN

*T*he kitchen of this country manor house is a family room used constantly by adults and children of all ages, their toys and their dogs. Instead of choosing a dull carpet or terracotta tiles for the floor, shiny, hand-made white tiles were laid. Far from being difficult to clean, the glossy surface just needs a quick wipe with a cloth to remove paw prints and muddy boot marks. The white walls in this well-used room need touching up with fresh paint occasionally and this can be done just in the affected areas without the whole room needing to be re-painted.

The fabrics chosen needed to work in the bright sunlight and on dull, wintry days, so yellow was chosen as the major color, in a bold check to balance the white. Slipcovers (loose covers) for easy cleaning are fitted over the sofas and chairs, which were first upholstered in muslin (calico). The theme of yellow and blue is repeated in different tones, with the accessory colors of terracotta, green, turquoise blue, and a little bright ocher adding interest and contrast.

COUNTRY BEDROOM

*T*his sophisticated bedroom has been furnished entirely in neutral colors accented with black to create a strong, masculine environment. This combination of metal, geometrics, and stripes could easily have become formal and too harsh for a bedroom, but the fabrics chosen and construction methods used have instead given the room richness of texture, and softness of line without the need for any other colors.

The ties at the bed curtains, the sweep of the window curtains, the softness of the shade (blind), and the duvet headboard all diffuse the strength of the black stripes which could have been dominant.

The campaign sofa is upholstered in off-white canvas to be as simple as possible against the lines of the metal and to contrast with the blousy bed curtains. The simple print on the shades (blinds) softens the window edges, to frame the wonderful views from each window along the valley to either side of the farmhouse.

To set the atmosphere for the room, the dense velvet pile carpet contrasts beautifully with the

rough, washed paint effect of the walls. The firm texture and simplicity of the ticking stripe used for the bedcurtains (and lining of the main curtains) complements the damask bedcover. The elegant moiré stripe used for the throws and cushions and the elegant woven striped damask of the window curtains give extra dimension to the draped fabrics. The upholstered tables in damask keep the bed area as a single unit, while the black and tan weave used on the end of bed stool identifies the proportions of the bed and the metal framework.

A colorful kilim rug has been added at the end of the bed for a complete contrast. This rug is not necessary to make the room "work" but does give the owner's dog a resting place.

The elegance and color scheme of this bedroom could place it as a stylish bachelor apartment in the center of a large city, but it is in fact in the heart of the countryside, perfectly in harmony with the surrounding acres of greenery, with the interplay of light from three windows adding a luxurious element unavailable in the city.

DRAWING ROOM

A contemporary painting, with the promise of more in similar vein to come, set the scene for this country drawing room. Although in an old rectory in a typical country setting overlooking lawns and herbaceous borders, we wanted a room that bore no resemblance to the over-designed "English Country House" look.

We decided to imitate the painting in essence and use strong colors to create a room that is comfortable, but unpredictable. Each piece of furniture is upholstered in a different color, using woven fabrics incorporating a damask weave and woven fine stripes in three other colors, a small medallion print in soft shades, a sharper geometric motif for the footstool/coffee table, and a rich, solid damask for the desk chair.

PERIOD ROOM

*T*his little country cottage was adapted last century during the revival of interest in the Gothic style. Consequently the windows and the woodwork details are Victorian Gothic, allowing rich textures and weaves to be used together – in fact demanding them. Carefully displayed collections of porcelain, pictures, books, and furnishings make this room a "little gem".

A large Persian rug fills the central floor area, and the button-back chair is upholstered in a multi-colored tapestry fabric with a double piping trim picking out one of the colors. The sofa is covered in a rich, tomato-colored, herringbone weave.

A footstool with a cushion attached, upholstered in a simple check, plus linen- and velvet-covered cushions, add understated details to the room. The window drapes, with their elaborate floral design, printed in deep reds, terracottas, and earth colors, provide the largest area of fabric and therefore represent the main theme of the room.

COMFORTABLE LIVING ROOM

*T*his room has been transformed from a rather uninteresting beige and brown room which always felt rather dull and inward-looking into a comfortable and restful living room. The country style furnishings and colors chosen for the redecoration blend with the soft green foliage outside, drawing the eye toward the window and thus to the outside, making the room feel larger and at one with its natural surroundings.

The wall and woodwork colors have been chosen for their combined qualities of depth and subtlety of tone. The natural seagrass flooring and pale checked Indian flat weave dhurrie keep the room simple, as do the curtains in natural canvas lined with a soft blue striped cotton. Carefully chosen simple checks and country prints have been used for the slipcovers (loose covers) and cushions, adding soft colors to the basic blue and green scheme.

FAMILY ROOM

The chairs and sofas in this family living room needed to be robust, but because the windows are situated at opposite sides, making this a very light room, the colors could not be dark. The basic colors are pink and coral in mid-tones. One sofa upholstered in a plain pink herringbone weave and the other in a printed chintz set the scene for the informality and color balance of the overall scheme. Other colors and prints are added by the tablecloths and cushions in pale olive greens, soft blues, and yellows. An Aubusson-style, crewelwork rug repeats those colors already used in a different context, and adds some "older" colors to balance the others.

The bold tartan upholstery of the central stool prevents the room from being too pastel and is integrated with the rest of the furniture through the matching throws on the sofa.

STUDY BEDROOM

*T*he cobalt blue walls chosen for this room balance the bright red/pink checked curtains perfectly. Upholstering the chair and window seat in strong browny-taupe colors prevents the room from becoming too predictable and counterbalances the other two colors. Fabrics in three different colors in different checks and stripes have been skillfully combined with a simple two-toned design which is just floral enough to add informality without being too "chintzy".

The colors have been used quite separately, but repeated around the room to give a unity which both pleases the senses and holds the design together. The red of the curtains has been repeated in a slightly stronger tone and pattern on the headboard, the taupe coloring has been used on the bed as a dust ruffle (valance), on the window seat and again on the chair, but each time in a different pattern. The attention to detail, such as the red buttons on the window seat, adds a touch of formality but this effect has been used sparingly so that it does not dominate the overall decorative style of the room.

The simplicity of the coloring and the careful balance of scale and tone in each of the fabrics, combined with the painted and plain wood country furniture, make this room comfortable to work in and relaxing to sleep in.

TOWNHOUSE BEDROOM

The lovely hand-stitched wool on cotton crewelwork curtains are central to this bedroom. Colorings in soft tones of pinks, blues, and green have soft taupes and beiges running through them to add depth. Cream and deep cream wallpaper in a simple stripe allows the delicate colors of the fabrics to set the tone of the room without competition.

The bed is simply dressed with a stylized, aqua-blue, floral fabric on an off-white ground which echoes the crewelwork design. Combining this print with fine striped lining, simply edged in blue, and with white and off-white bedlinen prevents the canopy from dominating the room. A log cabin patchwork quilt picks out the colors used around the room. The fabric-covered end-of-bed stool provides a handy surface. To complete the walls, a delicately hand-painted and stenciled rose border has been added.

An upholstered modern chair in plain green and a button-back armchair in pink take up the color theme without complicating the design.

THE
WORKROOM

THE WORKROOM

*I*f you have enough space to set aside one room as a permanent workroom, construct a good worktable (see below) to fit in the middle of the room with space to walk around all sides.

Under the table have two shelves for materials – fabric rolls, interlining, lining, etc. Along one wall build a bench, so that large pieces of fabric can lie flat or small items can be made up without disturbing the work on the main table.

Fit in a table for the sewing machine against another wall, and have plenty of shelving against a third wall for storing books, notes, fabric samples, and small pieces of equipment.

THE WORKTABLE

The ideal size for a worktable is 10 × 5 ft (3 × 1.5 m), allowing long curtains to lie flat on the length of the table and whole widths of fabric to fit across it. Having enough space to walk all around the table allows marking and cutting to be done without moving the fabric.

Cover the top with a layer of interlining and a top cover of muslin (calico) or curtain lining. Staple securely to the underside. This will give you a surface which can be pinned into and pressed on, which will hold the fabrics flat, and which will be comfortable to work on.

If space is limited, the size of the table can be reduced to 8 × 4 ft (2.5 × 1.25 m) and one end can be put against a wall.

If you do not have a permanent work space, a temporary top can be made for your dining table using a sheet of 8 × 4 ft (2.5 × 1.25 m) particleboard or plywood, cut in half and hinged to fold away, with wooden blocks on the underside, so that it will not move against the table. The whole underside should be covered in heavy-duty felt to prevent any damage to the table top.

The minimum size for an upholstery worktable is 6 × 4 ft (1.6 × 1.3 m), with a frame solid enough to take the weight of a chair.

TOOLS AND THEIR USES

Tack hammer
This is magnetic at one end of the head, so that the tack will stick to the hammer, leaving the hand free to hold the fabric.

Blunt chisel and mallet
Used to strip off the old upholstery.

Stapler
Buy a stapler which will take $\frac{1}{4}$ in (6 mm) and $\frac{3}{8}$ in (10 mm) staples.

Staple remover
A special tool for removing staples – a screwdriver can also be used for the same purpose.

Webbing stretcher
Canvas webbing is applied under tension using this tool.

Curved needles
For stitching awkward angles, available in 2 in (5 cm) and 4 in (10 cm) sizes.

Buttoning needle
Used to stitch buttons to upholstered furniture and to stitch right through an upholstery pad to secure it to the webbing and burlap (hessian).

Stuffing regulator
A long needle with points at both ends, used to pull stuffing forward when sewing the firm edge around a seat (known as the edge roll) and to redistribute lumpy areas of stuffing.

1 strong thread
2 twine
3 spring twine (laidcord)
4 canvas webbing
5 back tack strip
6 springs
7 tacks
8 button forms
9 zips
10 sewing threads
11 piping cord
12 snapper strip

1 heavyweight unbleached interlining
2 sarille (synthetic) interlining
3 canvas
4 lightweight bleached interlining
5 white curtain lining
6 cream curtain lining
7 muslin (calico)
8 black twill
9 barrier cloth
10 foam in different densities
11 coir fiber
12 horsehair
13 cotton batting (wadding)
14 lightweight burlap (hessian)
15 heavy-duty burlap (hessian)
16 polyester batting (wadding)

Clamps
For woodwork repairs.

Craft knife
For cutting strings and twines when removing springs, etc.

Pincers
For pulling out broken tacks and staples.

Sewing machine
You will need a sturdy, basic machine with forward and reverse stitches. A swing needle may be useful but is not essential. The three feet you will need are: normal stitching foot, piping foot, and zipper foot.

Iron
Use the heaviest domestic steam iron possible. Keep it filled with water to maximize the weight. It should be able to reach a high temperature and to have steam and spray controls.

Ruler
A yardstick (meter ruler) is needed for measuring fabric and accurate lengths.

Seam (marker) gauge
A small 6–7 in (15–18 cm) ruler with a marker that can be set is also useful, to ensure accurate hems and seam allowances.

Tape measure
Use linen or other non-stretching material.

Carpenter's (set) square
At least 24 × 12 in (60 × 30 cm). Use for squaring fabric sides and hems.

Scissors
(1) For cutting, use large, heavy scissors with 8–9 in (20–23 cm) blades.
(2) For trimming, have a small pair with 3–4 in (7.5–10 cm) blades.

Seam ripper (quick-unpick)
For mistakes!!

Point turner (plioir)
A plastic or bone tool for creasing and turning points, when covering

cardboard with fabric or fitting fabric linings into drawers.

Threads
Match like for like where possible: cotton or cotton-wrapped polyester thread with cotton (and wool) fabric, silk thread to silk fabric, etc.

Pin cushions
Have a large pin cushion for use on the worktable and a small wrist pin cushion to use when at the sewing machine and away from the table.

Pins
Fine steel $1\frac{3}{8}$ in (35 mm) medium weight, for general use. Use 2 in (50 mm) heavy pins for loose covers and heavy fabrics.

Needles
Available in many sizes: "sharps" for medium to fine fabric, "betweens" for medium to heavy fabric.

Upholstery skewers
Use upholstery skewers to hold heavy fabrics in place.

Thimble
Essential to protect fingers when working with several layers of fabric and very heavy fabrics.

Curtain clips
Use large bulldog clips to hold the fabrics to the table, to prevent the fabrics moving until stitched.

Marking pen
Use a marking pen with ink that can be washed out. Always test on a sample of your fabric.

MATERIALS AND THEIR USES

Canvas webbing
Strips of tightly woven fabric which form the base on which all the other upholstery materials are built.

Burlap (hessian)
Heavy-duty to go over webbing and springs;
lightweight to cover hair or coir fiber to make pads for arms, backs, and seats.

Barrier cloth
If the top fabric does not meet the legal requirements for flame-resistance in the U.K., barrier cloth should be upholstered onto a piece of furniture before the top fabric.

Coir fiber
Less expensive stuffing used for padding.

Horsehair
Natural stuffing used in traditional upholstery.

Fire-retardant foam
Foam is readily available in a range of thicknesses in $\frac{1}{4}$ in (5 mm) multiples from $\frac{1}{4}$ in (5 mm) to 4 in (10 cm). Always ask your supplier's advice when choosing foam for a particular project.

Always use foam which has been specially treated for fire resistance.

Tacks
These come in various sizes:
– 1 in (25 mm) used when tying springs;
– $\frac{1}{2}$ in (13 mm) used on webbing and heavy-duty burlap (hessian);
– $\frac{3}{8}$ in (10 mm) used to keep hair pads, muslin (calico), underlinings, and top covers in place;
– $\frac{1}{4}$ in (6 mm) used for delicate fabrics or thin wood.

Gimp pins
Used to attach braids and top covers where the tacks are to show. They come in various colors.

Heavy-duty spring twine (known as laidcord)
Used to tie down springs.

Twine
Used to sew springs in place and for other internal sewing.

Strong thread
Used to sew top covers invisibly where tacks would show, or where there is no wood into which tacks can be hammered.

Springs
These come in various sizes, shapes, and gauges (see page 14).

Polyester or Dacron batting (wadding)
Used over foam to prevent the foam from rubbing against the top fabric and to cover staples.

Linterfelt or cotton batting (wadding)
An interlining used on traditional upholstery under the muslin (calico) and for padding hard edges, e.g. ottoman sides. Also called "bump" – available as lightweight, mediumweight and heavyweight. Best in 95–100% cotton.

Sarille interlining
A synthetic interlining approximately half the price of the cotton ones. Sarille will flatten in time. Use for padding flat cushions if cotton interlining is unavailable.

Black twill
Use as "cambric" or platform cloth for chair seats, under seats instead of burlap (hessian), and as headboard backs instead of muslin (calico).

Curtain lining
Available in various qualities and colors. Do not compromise on the quality. Neutral colors – cream, white, and beige – are most used in upholstery.

Muslin (calico)
Use to make patterns for slipcovers (loose covers) and in upholstery to hold hair or fiber in place.

Twill (India) tape
Used for ties under slipcovers (loose covers) for chairs, available in $\frac{1}{2}$ in (13 mm) or 1 in (25 mm) widths.

Snapper strip
Use as an alternative to zippers at the back of box cushions.

Piping cord
Comes in various sizes (see page 18):
– $\frac{1}{4}$ in (no. 6), use for heavy fabrics or if you want the cording to stand out;
– $\frac{1}{6}$ in (no. 4), for normal use;
– $\frac{1}{20}$ in (no. 1), a tiny cord for narrow piping on edges and bows.

Zipper
White and beige are the standard colors used unless a specific color match is required. Use as a closure for cushions of all kinds but not for slipcovers (loose covers).

Back tack strip
Use to hold fabrics in place and produce a neat foldline, e.g. to attach the top fabric at the back of a chair.

Glue
Wood glue for frame repairs; fabric glue (liquid rubber) to attach braids.

Wood preservative
For the treatment of woodworm.

Wood polishes
These should be pure wax and not contain silicone, which eventually clogs the grain. Polish can be bought with color added to match the wood.

Mineral spirits (white spirit) and the finest steel (wire) wool
For cleaning wood.

Sandpaper
For rubbing down frames.

GLOSSARY OF FABRICS

Batik
Batik cloths are named after the Malay resist-dyeing method used to make the pattern on the fabric. The designs are drawn onto the woven cloth in wax or a similar substance. The cloth is then dyed in various colors, which do not penetrate the waxed areas, thus producing the characteristic patterns.

Brocade
Brocade is traditionally woven fabric using silk, cotton, wool, or mixed fibers on a jacquard loom, in a multi- or self-colored floral design. Traditional motifs such as cherubs, vases, ribbons, bunches of flowers, etc., are mixed together. A true brocade is based on one or two basic colors with additional colored weft threads which float on the back and are brought forward to the front to produce the pattern on the right side. Sometimes metal threads are used to give an extra dimension to the design.

Heavier than damask, brocade is used for traditional upholstery, and goes especially well with gilt framed chairs or polished wood. Often used as wall lining in stately homes with gilt filet all around.

Brocatelle
Has raised areas of pattern formed by the use of a double warp. Woven in a satin or twill design on either a plain or a satin ground, in one or two colors.

Burlap (hessian)
A coarse, plain, fabric woven from jute or jute and hemp, in various weights. Usually washable – but wash before making up to check shrinkage. Can be dyed in many colors. Use for sacking, and in traditional upholstery.

Cambric
Made from linen or cotton, a closely woven, plain weave fabric with a sheen on one side. Use, wash, and press as for muslin (calico). Cambric is widely used for cushion pad covers as the close weaves prevent feathers creeping through.

Canvas
Often called "cotton duck": a plain weave cotton in various weights. Available as unbleached, coarse cotton or more finely woven and dyed in strong colors. Canvas will not have been treated for use on furnishings, so will need washing first to shrink thoroughly. It is easy to dye and will take stenciled and hand-painted designs well. Suitable for upholstered chair covers, slipcovers, awnings, and outdoor use.

Chenille
A half-velvet cloth, less expensive to produce than velvet. Chenille has long been used for table coverings and portiere curtains. Use for cushions and throws, or to upholster headboards and occasional chairs.

Chintz
Traditionally a cotton fabric with an Eastern design using flowers and birds, often with a resin finish which gave a characteristic sheen (glaze) and which repelled dirt. Now mostly used to

describe any patterned or plain glazed fabric. The glaze will eventually wear off and will wash out.

Corduroy

A strong cotton fabric woven to form vertical ribs by floating extra yarns across which are then cut to make the pile. Press on a velvet pinboard while still damp. Use for traditional upholstery.

Crewel

A plain or hopsack weave, natural cotton ground embroidered in chain stitch in plain cream or multi-colored wools. Formerly crewelwork was hand-embroidered by the lady of the house into bedcovers and hangings; now it is mostly handmade in India in floral and Eastern designs.

Damask

A jacquard fabric first woven in Damascus in Syria, which was the center of the silk trade. White linen damask cloths were first recorded in the 16th century at the tables of royalty. Huguenots fleeing from France in the 17th century went to Ireland and there made linen damask. First woven in silk, with satin floats on a satin warp background; now woven in linen, cotton or wool, or mixed fibers in various weights. Most damasks are self colored. The surface design runs in a different direction from the background and the face cloth has a sheen. Damask cloths can be made up reversed if a matte finish is required. May be dry-cleaned or washed depending on the fiber content.

Different weights need to be chosen for different uses. Heavy damask is suitable for traditional upholstery.

Gaufraged velvet

Gaufraging can be done to any good quality velvet (see below). A design is pressed (branded) into the pile, by heated metal cylinders with designs carved into them.

Gingham

A plain weave fabric with equal width stripes of white plus one other color in both warp and weft threads to produce checks. Usually 100% cotton or a cotton blend. Use for cushions and slipcovers (loose covers) in cottage-style rooms, kitchens, or children's bedrooms.

Ikat

First developed in Indonesia, the traditional ikat pattern is formed by weaving threads which have been resist-dyed. Strands of yarn are bound together tightly at chosen intervals and the bundle is dyed. The bound sections do not absorb the dye. The yarns are then untied and retied and dyed in another color and so on. The yarn is then woven into a flat weave. The fuzzy outlines of the resulting geometric designs are characteristic of these weaves.

Use for cushions and slipcovers (loose covers).

Indiennes or French provincial prints

During the mid-17th century some Parisians imported richly printed cloths ("toiles peintes") from India. By 1675 Nîmes and Avignon had thriving businesses printing "les Indiennes" (small, colorful patterns) by hand onto muslin (calico), using carved blocks, also imported from India. The colors were all created using natural dyes and the distinctive designs were soon adapted for decorative home accessories.

Kilim

Kilims are flatweave Persian rugs, mainly wool but sometimes in silk or cotton, always with bold, simple patterns. The colors are woven in such a way that there are slits left, which are joined up the next time that particular color is used. Kilim rugs have become popular in the last decade for use as the top cover fabric when upholstering sofas and chairs.

Lampas

Similar to a damask weave, with areas of unblended color created by using extra warp and weft threads in patterned areas.

Lisere

Made as lampas but with additional striped bands of warped threads in the main cloth.

Moiré

A finish usually on silk or acetate, described as "water-marked". The characteristic moiré markings are produced by pressing plain woven fabric through hot, engraved cylinders which crush the threads and push them into different directions to form the pattern. This is not a permanent finish and will disappear on contact with water. Because these markings are not durable, upholstery fabrics are often made with a jacquard moiré design woven in.

Moquette

A very hard-wearing cloth, usually cotton, sometimes wool. The pattern is made during the weaving. Half of the pile threads are looped over wires to form areas of raised design. The resulting fabric is bulky and difficult to stretch around curves. Use on larger rather than smaller pieces of upholstery. Popular in the 1950s and making a comeback now.

Muslin (calico)

A coarse, plain weave cotton in cream or white with "natural" flecks in it. Available in many widths and weights depending on the quality of the cotton used. To ensure the fabric is fully shrunk, wash before use and press while damp, as it creases easily. This fabric was and still is used as the base cloth for printing.

Use as a cover for padding in traditional upholstery and as a pattern for slipcovers (loose covers).

Organdy

The very finest cotton fabric usually from Switzerland. An acid finish gives organdy a unique crispness. Washable, but needs to be pressed damp. Use for lightweight dressing table curtains, perhaps over a colored lining. Organdy can also be used to make lovely pleated and butterfly ruffled (frilled) edgings.

Ottoman
A heavy cotton or cotton blend fabric woven in such a way as to form horizontal ribs. Extra weft cords are covered by the warp threads. A stiff fabric suitable for upholstery.

Plaid
Wool or worsted cloth in square or rectangular checked designs as in tartans (see below). Usually woven in two to three colors, often used for shawls or more tightly woven for men's sports clothes. Use to upholster stools, fenders, chairs, or sofas.

Printed stripes
Printing rather than weaving stripes allows flat woven cottons to become elegant rather than "chintzy" at a lower cost than woven stripe. The design will always lack the depth of a woven cloth, but sometimes the sheen which can be incorporated in the finishing makes up for this and a richness is added that textured weaves cannot give. Stripes are often wanted without having to use a heavyweight fabric, and printed stripes are perfect in these situations.

Sailcloth
A very stiff, hard-wearing fabric in plain or basket weave in cotton or cotton/polyester blend. Iron while damp, as sailcloth creases easily. Most useful in creamy white for furnishings or colored and striped for garden awnings and deck chairs.

Silk noil
Light to medium weight silk in a natural color with small pieces of the silk moth's cocoon woven in as flecks. Relatively inexpensive. Use for slipcovers (loose covers) and cushions.

Silk shantung
Light to medium weight silk woven with irregular yarns giving a dull, rough appearance. Available in an extensive range of colors. Gathers well for very feminine treatments and finishes. Use for cushions.

Taffeta
Originally woven from silk, now also in acetate and blends. A plain weave fabric with a light-catching sheen resulting from the fibers used. Interesting checked patterns can be made by weaving varying hues and tones of colors together. Use for flat and box cushions, especially for bedrooms.

Tapestry
Traditionally a multicolored, hand-woven fabric depicting historical and pastoral scenes. Now used to describe heavy, stiff fabrics machine-woven in several layers to produce a durable fabric.

Machine-woven tapestry, although not as hard-wearing as the real thing, has greater flexibility and can be used to upholster sofas, chairs, boxes, and ottomans. The designs and good colorings make this textile an attractive proposition for many upholstery uses.

Tartan
Authentic tartans are woven or worsted, fine twill weaves with elaborate checked designs, which belong to individual Scottish clans or families. Both warp and weft have threads of mixed colors. Tartan designs are now also woven in silk to produce elegant, shimmering fabrics. Wool tartans are hard-wearing and suitable for upholstering sofas and chairs, and for cushion covers.

Ticking
Originally a fine, striped, woven linen used for covering feather mattresses, since its characteristic tight herringbone weave repels feathers. Traditionally in black and white, ticking is now woven in many colors and weights. Not usually pre-shrunk. Use as a lining for blanket chests and suitcases, and for slipcovers (loose covers) and cushions of all kinds.

Toile de Jouy
Created in France in 1770, this fabric features pastoral designs in one color printed on muslin (calico) cloth from India using copper plate printing techniques. Use for slipcovers (loose covers), upholstery, and cushions. Use throughout a room or on a small piece of period upholstery. Different patterns and colorways can be mixed together very effectively.

Velvet
Originally 100% silk, now made from cotton, viscose, or other man-made fibers. Velvet is woven as a double cloth each with its own warp and weft, with a distance of approximately $\frac{1}{4}$ in (6 mm) between them. The pile is woven between the two cloths, then a knife fitted to a metal roller cuts the pile, and the two cloths are rolled away from each other onto separate drums.

Care needs to be taken when sewing or the fabrics will "walk". Always press on a pinboard. Dry clean carefully. Always buy a good velvet with a dense pile which will not pull out easily. Inexpensive velvet will gradually flatten on upholstery and the pile will wear away. For these reasons, never be tempted to use the less expensive curtain velvet for upholstery.

The following lists contain details of the fabrics shown in the photographs in chapter 9. The textile company's name is given first followed by the name of the fabric design.

page 154 (left)
Clockwise from bottom right hand corner:
Pierre Frey – Les Paniers Fleuris
Designers Guild – Marquetry
Manuel Canovas – Vitry
Percheron – Strie
Jane Churchill – Celandine
Colefax and Fowler – Motcombe
Pierre Frey – Brigitte
Colefax and Fowler – Chester Check
Colefax and Fowler – Paris
Jane Churchill – Leaf
Colefax and Fowler – Burford Stripe

page 154 (right)
Clockwise from top left hand corner:
Marvic – Pine Tree
Jane Churchill – Leaf
Manuel Canovas – Camila
Gainsborough – Damask
Colefax and Fowler – Maybury
Colefax and Fowler – Starweave
Jane Churchill – Leaf
Colefax and Fowler – Banbury
Colefax and Fowler – Dalmation
Jane Churchill – Damask

page 155 (left)
Clockwise from bottom left hand corner:
Colefax and Fowler – Starweave
Pierre Frey – Les Paniers Fleuris
Parkertex – Frou-Frou
Colefax and Fowler – Banbury
Turnell & Gigon – Check
Marvic – Vermont
Jane Churchill – Celandine
Colefax and Fowler – Paris
Colefax and Fowler – Strawberry Leaf
Pierre Frey – Cap Ferrat

page 155 (right)
Clockwise from top left hand corner:
Colefax and Fowler – Chester Check
Manuel Canovas – Tremolat
Colefax and Fowler – Motcombe
Nobilis Fontan – Grande Plaine

Manuel Canovas – Passy
Colefax and Fowler – Hazelmere
Pierre Frey – Les Paniers Fleuris
Colefax and Fowler – Stratford
Pierre Frey – Brigitte
Colefax and Fowler – Tavistock

page 156 (left)
Clockwise from bottom left hand corner:
Pallu and Lake – Dresden
Pierre Frey – Barbizon
Gainsborough – Silk Taffeta
Parkertex – My Lady's Garden
Gainsborough – Damask
Nobilis Fontan – Porporino
Calluna – White Crewelwork
Warner – Georgian Stripe
Gainsborough – Damask
Muslin (Calico)
Gainsborough – Damask

page 156 (right)
Clockwise from top left hand corner:
Percheron – Strie
Pierre Frey – Srinagar
The Isle Mill – Traditional Tartan
Daniel Hechter – Berkeley
Calluna – Derby
Parkertex – Frou-Frou

page 157 (left)
Clockwise from top left hand corner:
Calluna – Piona
Manuel Canovas – Tremolat
Manuel Canovas – Vitry
Calluna – Piona
Alton-Brooke – Gingham Check
Colefax and Fowler – Caroline
Pierre Frey – Brigitte

page 157 (right)
Clockwise from bottom left hand corner:
Daniel Hechter – Berkeley
Colefax and Fowler – Hazelmere
Mulberry – Ikat Check
Daniel Hechter – Berkeley
Manuel Canovas – Passy
Pierre Frey – Brigitte

page 158
Clockwise from the top of the star:
Colefax and Fowler – Banbury
Bennison – Oak Leaf
Manuel Canovas – Camila

Marvic – Tulipan
Nobilis Fontan – Grande Plaine
Guy Evans – Fleurettes
Jane Churchill – Celandine
Marvic – Pine Tree
Les Olivades – Indianaire
Colefax and Fowler – Tavistock

page 159
Clockwise from the top of the star:
Pierre Frey – Brigitte
Guy Evans – 1182-01
Jane Churchill – Karlsen Stripe
Brunschwig & Fils – 4580-3
Charles Hammond – Boulogne
Pierre Frey – Marcilly
Zoffany – Hertford Stripe
Calluna – Green Ticking
Jane Churchill – Karlsen Check
Guy Evans – 1254-16

page 160
Clockwise from the top of the star:
Colefax and Fowler – Roses and Pansies
Colefax and Fowler – Longford
Charles Hammond – Fishing Party
Souleiado – Fleurs d'Arles
Colefax and Fowler – Hampton
Souleiado – Fleurs d'Arles
Calluna – Piona
Charles Hammond – Fishing Party
Colefax and Fowler – Boughton
Charles Hammond – Aldwych

page 161
Clockwise from the top of the star:
Mulberry – Paisley Chenille
Manuel Canovas – Camila
Turnell & Gigon – 1T1021-141
Manuel Canovas – Acer
Manuel Canovas – Hyderabad
Manuel Canovas – Romanoff
Pierre Frey – Langeais
Manuel Canovas – Pomone
D G Distribution – Briseide
Manuel Canovas – Calinou

page 162
Clockwise from the top of the star:
Manuel Canovas – Tcheou
Colefax and Fowler – Paris
Percheron – Rosemire
Manuel Canovas – Tremolat

Colefax and Fowler – Paris
Colefax and Fowler – Star
Pierre Frey – Marcilly
Pierre Frey – Freyline
Manuel Canovas – Tcheou
Colefax and Fowler – Felbrigg

page 163
Clockwise from the top of the star:
Marvic – Pine Tree
Beaumont & Fletcher – Fig Leaf
MRH Cloth – Pomegranate
Bennison – All Over
Bennison – Oak Leaf
Bennison – Lion Column
Bennison – Turkish Star
Charles Hammond – Boulogne
Bennison – Faded Roses
Abbot & Boyd – Passion

A d d r e s s e s ───────────

**Where no other address is shown
contact the U.K. office for the
nearest stockist.**

ABBOT & BOYD 88 Garlands Road,
    Redhill, Surrey RH1 6NZ, U.K. Tel:
    0737 799321
ALTON-BROOKE 5 Sleaford Street,
    London SW8 5AB, U.K. Tel: 071 622
    9372
BEAUMONT & FLETCHER 134 Lots
    Road, London SW10 0RJ, U.K. Tel:
    071 351 4333
Christopher Hyland Inc, D & D
    Building, Suite 1706, 979 Third
    Avenue, New York, NY 10022,
    U.S.A.
Cheshire Pty Ltd, 120 Union Road,
    Surrey Hills, 3127 Victoria,
    Australia
BENNISON 16 Holbein Place, London
    SW1W 8NL, U.K. Tel: 071 730 8076
Bennison Fabrics, 76 Greene Street,
    New York, NY 10012, U.S.A.
Michael Love, 72A New Beach Road,
    Darling Point, Sydney, NSW 2027,
    Australia

CALLUNA Hill House, Creech St
    Michael, Taunton, Somerset TA3
    5DP, U.K. Tel: 0823 443335
CHARLES HAMMOND (c/o Pallu &
    Lake)
COLEFAX & FOWLER 118 Garratt
    Lane, London SW18 4DJ, U.K. Tel:
    081 874 6484
Cowtan & Tout, 979 Third Avenue, New
    York, NY 10022, U.S.A.
Colefax & Fowler Pty, 46 Queen Street,
    Woollahra, Sydney, NSW 2025,
    Australia
DANIEL HECHTER (c/o Parkertex)
DESIGNERS GUILD 271 & 277 Kings
    Road, London SW3 5EN, U.K. Tel:
    071 351 5775
Wardlaw Pty Ltd, 230–232 Auburn
    Road, Hawthorn, Melbourne,
    Victoria 3122, Australia
D G DISTRIBUTION 26 Old Church
    Street, London SW3 5BY, U.K. Tel:
    071 352 3111
GAINSBOROUGH SILK WEAVING
    COMPANY Alexandra Road,
    Chilton, Sudbury, Suffolk, U.K. Tel:
    0787 372081
GUY EVANS 51A Cleveland Street,
    London W1P 5PQ, U.K. Tel: 071 436
    7914
JANE CHURCHILL (c/o Colefax &
    Fowler)
LES OLIVADES 7 Walton Street,
    London SW3 1JD, U.K. Tel: 071 589
    8990
Provençal Imports, 8841 Beverley
    Boulevard, Los Angeles, CA 90048,
    U.S.A.
Provençal Fabrics, 2 Transvaal Avenue,
    Double Bay, Sydney, Australia
MANUEL CANOVAS 2 North Terrace,
    Brompton Road, London SW3 2BA,
    U.K. Tel: 071 225 2298
D & D Building, 979 Third Avenue,
    New York, NY 10022, U.S.A.
Order Imports, 11A Boundary Street,
    Rushcutters Bay, Sydney, NSW
    2011, Australia
MARVIC Unit 1, West Point Trading
    Estate, Alliance Road, Acton,

London W3 0RA, U.K. Tel: 081 993
    0191
MULBERRY AT HOME The Rookery,
    Chilcompton, Nr Bath, BA3 4EH,
    U.K. Tel: 0761 232855
Lee Jofa, 800 Central Boulevard,
    Carlstadt, NJ 07072, U.S.A.
Albena Imports, 60 Moray Street, South
    Melbourne, Victoria 3205, Australia
NOBILIS FONTAN 1–2 Cedar Studios,
    45 Glebe Place, London SW3 5JE,
    U.K. Tel: 071 351 7878
PALLU & LAKE Springvale Terrace,
    London W14 0EA, U.K. Tel: 071 602
    7250
PARKERTEX P.O. Box 30, West End
    Road, High Wycombe, Bucks HP11
    2QD, U.K. Tel: 0494 71166
St James Furnishings Pty Ltd, 142–144
    Burwood Road, Hawthorn, 3122
    Victoria, Australia
H A PERCHERON 97–99 Cleveland
    Street, London W1P 5PN, U.K. Tel:
    071 580 1192
PIERRE FREY 253 Fulham Road,
    London SW3 6HY, U.K. Tel: 071 376
    5599
Fonthill, U.S.A. Tel: 212 755 6700
Wardlaw Pty, Australia Tel: Melbourne
    8194233
SOULEIADO 171 Fulham Road,
    London SW3 6JW, U.K. Tel: 071 589
    6180
THE ISLE MILL 12 West Moulin Road,
    Pitlochry PH16 5AF, Scotland Tel:
    0796 472390
TURNELL & GIGON Unit M20,
    Chelsea Garden Market, Chelsea
    Harbour, Lots Road, London SW10
    0XE, U.K. Tel: 071 351 5142
WARNER FABRICS Bradbourne
    Drive, Tilbrook, Milton Keynes MK7
    8BE, U.K. Tel: 0908 366900
Payne Fabrics, P.O. Box 983, Dayton,
    Ohio 45401, U.S.A.
Wardlaw Pty, 230–232 Auburn Road,
    Hawthorn, 3122 Victoria, Australia
ZOFFANY 63 South Audley Street,
    London W1Y 5BF, U.K. Tel: 071 629
    9262

INDEX